Table of Contents

INTRODUCTION 5

CHAPTER 1: IDENTIFYING A DIFFICULT PERSON 9

    IDENTIFYING A TOXIC PERSON 9

    NEGATIVITY 9

    ENVIOUS 10

    HUMILIATION 10

    DOMINEERING 10

    MANIPULATIVE 11

    OPPORTUNISTIC 11

    AGGRESSIVE 12

    SADISTIC AND UNSYMPATHETIC 12

    LYING AND EXAGGERATING 13

    FORM RATHER THAN SUBSTANCE 13

CHAPTER 2: CATEGORIES OF DIFFICULT PEOPLE AND IT'S CLASSIFICATIONS 15

    PERFECTIONISTS 15

    CONTROL FREAKS 24

    NARCISSISTS 31

    BULLIES 32

    SLACKERS 32

    PESSIMISTS 33

    THE HOSTILE OR BOSSY 33

    THE CHRONIC COMPLAINER 34

    THE SUPER-AGREEABLE 35

    CRITICS 36

CHAPTER 3: RESOLVING CONFLICTS 38

CHAPTER 4: EFFECTIVE PHRASES THAT CAN BE USED 53

CHAPTER 5: EFFECTIVE ATTITUDE 72
   Accepting the Limits 82
CHAPTER 6: CHANGING YOUR ENVIRONMENT 90
CHAPTER 7: THE "ANTI-DIFFICULT PEOPLE" TOOLKIT AND HOW TO LEARN FROM IT 109
   The "Anti-Difficult People" Toolkit 109
   Learning from Difficult People 113
CHAPTER 8: EXPERT TECHNIQUES TO DEAL WITH DIFFICULT PEOPLE 116
CONCLUSION 128

HOW TO DEAL WITH DIFFUCULT PEOPLE:

ESTABLISH EFFECTIVE RELATIONSHIPS WITH CHALLENGING PERSONALITIES BY DEALING WITH DIFFICULT SITUATIONS WITH PERSUASION TECHNIQUES. IMPROVE YOUR HUMAN RELATIONS TODAY

© Copyright 2020 - All rights reserved.

The content contained within this book may not be reproduced, duplicated or transmitted without direct written permission from the author or the publisher.

Under no circumstances will any blame or legal responsibility be held against the publisher, or author, for any damages, reparation, or monetary loss due to the information contained within this book. Either directly or indirectly.

Legal Notice:

This book is copyright protected. This book is only for personal use. You cannot amend, distribute, sell, use, quote or paraphrase any part, or the content within this book, without the consent of the author or publisher.

Introduction

Are there difficult people in your life? I guess that's why you are here. If you have not encountered difficult people before, then it is high time you start preparing for when that happens – because it will!

The thing with difficult people is that they often defy logic. Unfortunately, some of them are blissfully unaware of the kind of damage their attitude has on the people around them. Others are aware of the negative impact their actions cause but yet choose to derive their satisfaction from stirring up chaos and pushing people's buttons hard to know how far they can go. Whichever the case, their actions create unnecessary complexity, stress, and strife.

I run a business where we have over 200 employees. As we collaborate on various projects from time to time, there are instances where we encounter difficulties in getting a unanimous agreement on something because each member of the team is strongly opinionated. When I just started the company, I used to get bothered and so worked up in such situations. Each time I'd think, "Why are these people too difficult to deal with? What an irresponsible group...I don't even want to work with them anymore; I will fire them all!"

After some time, I realized that difficult people are everywhere. Even at home, I was dealing with a difficult teenage daughter who thought that she knew everything, and nothing you told her made any sense at all! The truth is, no matter where you are at or where you go, you will never be able to hide from such people. While it might be possible to avoid the first 1 or 2 of them, what of the 3rd, 5th, ….nth ones out there that you have not met yet? Avoiding these people is not a permanent solution unless you are willing to quit your job or move away from your home and never have anyone around you.

I don't know about you – but I think that this is not possible! Instead of running each time and trying to find solace where you will never find it, why not learn some incredible skills that will help you survive difficult people with so much ease and grace?

According to research, it is evident that difficult people can cause those around them stress. What is even more disturbing is the fact that fear has been shown to have a lasting negative impact on the human brain. When you are exposed to stress even just for a few days, the effectiveness of the neurons in your hippocampus – the part of the brain that is responsible for memory and reason – becomes compromised. If the stress goes on for several months, then the neurons are likely to get damaged. In other words, anxiety is one of the formidable threats to achieving success. If it gets out of control, then the chances are that your performance is affected.

The good news is that some of the common causes of stress are very easy to identify. For instance, if your company is working towards getting a grant for you to function, there is a high chance that you will feel stressed and learn how to manage it. However, when the source of stress is unexpected, then chances are that it will take you by surprise, and this is what causes the most harm.

According to research from the Department of Clinical and Biological Psychology, Friedrich Schiller University, and exposure to a stimulus that causes a negative emotion is the same as when one is exposed to difficult people. The two experiences cause one's brain to have a massive response to stress. In other words, when one is negative, crueler lazy, that alone is enough to drive the mind into a state of anxiety.

It is important to note that your ability to manage your emotional feelings and stay calm even when you are under so much pressure has a direct association with your performance. According to findings by Talent Smart, over 90% of top performers in any organization are skilled at managing their emotions during stress periods. What is interesting is that the reason why they have control over these stressful situations is that they have learned how to neutralize difficult people.

While there are several strategies, I have learned over the years from some of the top performers – who are my role models – on how to effectively deal with difficult people, I choose to share them here with you.

Keep reading!

Chapter 1: Identifying a Difficult Person

Identifying a Toxic Person

Now, let us look at the defining traits that are common to all types of toxic people. With these traits, you can identify the toxic people in your life and work on getting the toxicity out of your relationship.

Negativity

When anyone in your life is full of negativity, they are undoubtedly toxic. Yes, this trait alone is enough to make someone toxic. This is because of the effects that negativity can have on your life. If someone close to you sees your efforts as being incapable of yielding good results, you need to run from them. Negativity can be related in words, such as when Chloe told Nancy she was not cut out for law even though Nancy had won the award of best associate in the firm. Negativity can also come in deeds, such as when your brother, who had the opportunity to support you, refused to because he thought you were bound to fail in your endeavor, with no solid reason.

Envious

This is something that goes on in the mind but it may eventually leak through the cracks of the impulsive actions of the envious one, especially towards the envied. When, upon receiving a gift from your boyfriend, you caught an expressionless look on your friend's face, that may be the clue you need. When someone envies you for having something they do not have, their reaction to you will be that of scorn disguised as constructive criticism. Envy can serve as a very effective trigger for toxicity.

Humiliation

Humiliation, as a weapon in the arsenal of a toxic person, is employed when they try to be in control. If you prove yourself capable of seeing through them, through their ruse and façade, they will try to strip you of any dignity. This is to show you are no better than they are. Do not be surprised when they publicly use something you told them in confidence, against you, the same way John had used his knowledge of Bryan's medical history against him in a bar.

Domineering

As a feature of toxic people, expect them to want to lord it over you. It is an insatiable craving of theirs. Even when you stoop to the lowliest of points for them, they still are not satisfied. You need to be at their beck and call, to serve them, to satisfy them, to inconvenience yourself for them. If they are your boss, they have little regard for your dignity and overburden you with work, giving you the craziest of deadlines. These are deadlines that even they in their usual 'I-was-once-where-you-are-now" attitude cannot possibly meet. They want to feel in control and ensure they never lose grip on you.

Manipulative

This can come directly or indirectly. When it is direct, they appeal to your empathy, such as sobbing, crying, or emphasizing how much of a problem there will be if you do not do their bidding. When it is indirect, they appeal to your ego, your desire to be recognized and praised by them. They flatter you and put you on a high horse to nowhere. They string you out and leave you to dry.

Opportunistic

You are in business, and things are not going well for you. The banks have just called in the loans and all your assets, when sold, cannot even cover the interest, let alone the principal. You decide to initiate bankruptcy proceedings, but there is one concern: your mother's house used as collateral for the loan will be sold. You want that rich friend to buy the house, hold in some trust, and sell it back to you when things are good again. Of course, he has the means to even gift it to you. He agrees to it, and you facilitate his buying it. But when the time comes for him to transfer it back to you, he reneges on his promise. This friend is opportunistic. They secretly wish for your misfortune so that they can profit from it. Your case may not be a loan. It can be something as simple as their trying to take a position they knew you were wrongfully denied rather than trying to help you get it back.

Aggressive

Here, you must recall the bar fight between John and Bryan. The toxic people in your life resort to threats and force to get what they want from you or any other person. They are grown-up bullies whose desire to dominate other individuals forces them to do more than manipulate you. When you have suffered physical harm from a friend even once in unjustified aggression, the chances are that they are toxic and you should flee from them. The next time, you may not live to remember what happened, let alone reflect on it.

Sadistic and Unsympathetic

Some people enjoy being cruel to you just for fun. They derive pleasure from all the physical and mental torture they inflict on you. It pleases them to see you in pain, in anguish. They know, and they do not feel sorry for it, not even when you confront them about it. They keep coming back to you because they find you easy prey. Why go in search of another victim when here is the perfect one, you? These people are also insulated from feeling pity for you or from being able to imagine themselves in your shoes. They cannot do any of those because to them, it would be a sign of weakness.

Lying and Exaggerating

As a feature of toxicity, the borderline between these two, lying and exaggerating, becomes blurred. I am saying you find it difficult to tell when they are saying the truth because even when they are, they overstate it for reasons of invoking your pity or gaining your heightened admiration. Their lies can hurt you, mentally and physically: they make it difficult for you to trust them, to rely on them. Their exaggeration can confuse you, forcing you to act rashly. The simple truth is that they have no place in your life.

Form Rather than Substance

This is the toxic person's best way to wiggle out of ugly situations. They pay attention to form rather than substance. Imagine Ridley trying to discredit the two research papers because the publishers publish too many works yearly to be able to pay close attention to what they are publishing. Or imagine Chloe telling Nancy that if indeed she, Chloe, had done anything wrong, Nancy's reaction had made them even. All Nancy had said was, 'Chloe, I think we need to talk about us. I feel like we are not of great benefit to each other.'

The people in your life can possess any of the above traits to varying degrees. Any single one of them may be sufficient to declare someone as toxic. But pause a little bit. Why do you think you have toxic people in your life? Why do you find it difficult to evaluate any of your relationships and not find a John, a Ridley, or a Charlie in it? Could you be the problem? Could the problem be something else?

Chapter 2: Categories of Difficult People and It's Classifications

Perfectionists

When I first started my company, it used to take me at least 12 hours to produce an article that I thought was worthy of being published. My writers would send in their work, and I spent sleepless nights trying to edit and come up with the "perfect" piece. The thing with a perfectionist personality is that nothing will ever be good enough. You will find ways to look for mistakes, even where there aren't any.

One thing that is important to note is that being a perfectionist is something that is crippling. There may be that person in the office that is so passionate about their work is bursting with ideas but unfortunately cannot express them with unbridled freedom. It is the same thing with perfectionism – it holds you back because of anxiety, a sense of haunting unfulfillment, and depression.

Well, so many people think that being a perfectionist is about harboring the desire to be perfect alone. The truth is that it goes beyond that. You are merely choosing to derive your self-worth from the world around you. That explains why you end up being overly sensitive to criticism or rejection, and you end up believing that you are a stupid worthless failure or bad.

If you are a people-pleaser, then that is a sign of being a perfectionist. The thing is, seeking perfection often causes people anxiety because all they are thinking of is how they can be the best. You desire to control the outcome of your actions just so that you can gain approval, acceptance, praise, and rewards.

But do you think that the perfectionist in your office knows that they are obsessive and cynical in their behaviors? Certainly not! Just like I was, they may not even know that they are perfectionists, let alone putting in efforts to stop.

So, how do you deal with them?

Well, the thing with a perfectionist is that they are often detail-oriented, negative towards others, and sticklers for the rules. If your boss, subordinate, or colleague is this kind of person, the ways to handle them vary widely.

Dealing with a perfectionist subordinate

The thing that these people have in common is that they all notice details and have very high standards that an average person cannot even breath close. To deal with them, you must;

Avoid giving them large project scopes

One thing that is important to note is that most perfectionists have admirable qualities that many people find worthy. However, there are quite a few of them who choose to hone skills on a small component of a project instead of paying attention to the bigger picture. If you work with these kinds of people, it is helpful to assign them to select tasks based on their skillset.

In other words, you can opt to give them projects that are limited in scope but are detail-oriented. The truth is that most of them are not willing to delegate tasks, and the best thing you can do is allow them to work on projects independently – as long as the project requires a unified vision to complete.

Appeal to their sense of vanity and empathy

What if your employee is a neurotic or narcissistic perfectionist? Well, these kinds of people have a powerful desire to please others. The most effective way to motivate them is to explain to them how their style of work affects those in the team. Ensure that you phrase it in such a way that they realize you already know they have high standards – and that you appreciate these high standards they hold.

You may say things like, "Mary, you have very high standards, just like me. That is what this company is all about. However, remember that good morale is essential for good productivity."

What you are merely telling them is that the best way forward is to give a compliment even where they feel like there is something to criticize.

Appeal to their self-interest

What you will note is that several perfectionists want to be so perfect – either because of internal or external motivation. If you find that a subordinate is treating their colleagues poorly in the workplace just because they are perfectionists, remind them that such kind of people struggles hard to climb up the ladder. Remind them that the more they raise the ranks, the more they have to learn how to compromise for the sake of the whole team. Say something like, "I know you have been trying to ensure details of the project have been attended to, and the book does everything. That is great because if one is going to get the big things right, they will have to start by getting the little ones right. You are on the right track to the big things. However, what you need to remember as you progress is that the upper rank is about looking at the bigger picture. This means that if you focus too hard on getting 100% success, that will only bog you down. Have a vision for the next phase and not just a tunnel vision that might cost you more than you can pay for."

When you put it like that, they will start to realize that 100% is not all that counts, but achieving the primary goal, however, the approach you take is what counts at the end of the day.

When you are dealing with a perfectionist colleague, it is paramount that you know when to take a stand and when to let go. While this is something difficult to attain, you must take time to think about how important the issue at hand is so that you know when the time is right to take a stand.

The first thing is for you to keep a perspective. Agreeing with what your boss says does not mean that you have to follow their suggestions to the letter. While this seems at first as being passive, simply say yes and move on with your life. This will reduce the chances of stirring up conflict and stress. Saying yes to what they say does not mean that you have given away your power. It is quite the opposite because this will set you free from paying attention to their demands.

Ask them what it is they would like to do differently

Did you know that criticism is one of the best ways' perfectionists use to hide their insecurities? While this is upsetting, it always helps to remember that this is their defensive mechanism. They may just be lashing out because they feel insecure about one thing or the other.

When you take time to ask them what their preferred methods of going about something is, you are merely disarming those insecurities. Try telling them that you care about their emotions. When they realize that you understand their feelings, they will start to feel secure – and less critical in the future. Say things like, "I see that you are upset about the outcome of this project. Would you like a chance to talk about it?"

Stick to your guns

Think about it, is the issue you and your colleague have relevant? If so, then you are right to stick to your guns. There is a chance that no one at the office is aware that your colleague is a perfectionist. If there is something you consider relevant to you and disagree on, then realize that it is your right to spit it out.

Don't get me wrong- by disagreeing, I don't mean that you should argue about it. Simply state what it is that you disagree with and then move on. You don't have to let that disagreement to define the kind of relationship you both have. Simply say things like, "I understand where you are coming from. I just think that our perspectives are quite different on this one."

If they stir up an argument, simply walk away. No one will blame you for walking away from a case.

Keep distance

One of the simplest ways you can stay away from conflict is keeping a safe distance from it. If you have to work together on a project, simply remind them that each one of you has their roles and responsibilities and that you will do yours to your supervisor's satisfaction and not theirs.

You always have the choice of disengaging. If they keep going on and on about inconsequential details, all you have to do is remain noncommittal. Simply make your escape with such statements as "Huh, I didn't know you felt that way."

Dealing with a perfectionist supervisor

This is simply what I often refer to as 'managing up.' The main aim of doing this is to help you identify the personality of your boss – their strengths and weaknesses – so that you can effectively tailor your conversation to match theirs.

The problem with a perfectionist boss is that they always desire to be in charge. At first, this may be self-evident, but the truth is that it is not. Ask them what their expectations are. When you do this, you are giving them an enhanced feeling of being in control. This also protects you from providing an arbitrary response. While perfectionism may be unreasonable – inherently – you must try as much as possible not to be. The trick is for you to pay attention to their start points, endpoints, or boundaries to lower the chances of getting them angry.

Push information their way

Once you know what it is that your perfectionist boss is looking for, simply give them – don't wait until they ask for it. The more you offer them a wealth of information they are interested in, even before they can ask for it, the less likely they will think of you as a flawed person. This way, you escape conflict by being in the right place, at the right time doing the right thing. Remember, out of sight, out of mind!

Be at peace with the fact that there is only so much you can do

The fact that you are a subordinate means that you have very little influence on your superior's personality traits. There are times when they are critical and others overly-critical. But the good news is that you can still earn their trust and respect. The only downside to that is that you might have to endure too many interactions that are draining. Just do what is right and let the rest be decided by fate!

Seek mentorship and support elsewhere

Now, you have a perfectionist boss who is supposed to be your mentor, but the truth is that they have set unreasonable standards you cannot attain. This means that if you take them as mentors, you will strain yourself too much just to earn their praise.

Perfectionists make very poor mentors!

While we all need support at one point or another, you cannot find it from your perfectionist boss. The truth is that such people tend to hurt your self-image even more. The last thing you want is having your self-worth determined by people who already think that everyone but them is worthy.

Jump ship when you have to

Consider that dealing with such a boss is something that you have to adapt to and not accept it indefinitely. You must know when to cut the cord. The trick is for you to earn their recommendation and move on. This might mean that you seek employment elsewhere.

Start planning your exit strategy as early as you can.

Control Freaks

Let us consider the following situations;

You want to hang out with a friend you met recently, but then your long-term friend insists that you should not because you have not known them well enough to hang out with. This friend asks that if you are going to hang out, you must tell them where exactly you will be meeting when - date and time.

Does this sound familiar?

Well, the truth is that this has happened to us – whether by partners, friends, or family members.

Such kind of people is referred to as control freaks. Dealing with such types of people is not fun – no matter how much they mean to you. It could be that they are doing it because their heart is in the right place, or they mean you no harm, but this is entirely lethal force you don't want to mess with.

You may be thinking, but who exactly is a control freak? Well, a control freak simply refers to perfectionists who feel vulnerable to anything that seems to them as uncontrollable.

The term "control freak" is a psychology-related slang. It describes a person who wants to dictate what everyone does and how everything is done around them. People who have an extremely high need for control over others are considered as control freaks.

Their main attempt is to hide their vulnerabilities by ensuring that everything within their surroundings is under their control. They try hard to manipulate people and put so much pressure on them just so that they don't have to change themselves. Everywhere you go, you will spot a control freak – whether at home, school, or workplace.

With the right strategies up your sleeve, you can deal with them and live a happy life.

Get rid of turf wars

So many control freaks often feel the need to retain control of each aspect of their work just because they do not want to lose their status. It could be that there was a time when they were the only employee in the office and were used to doing all things by themselves. The problem with these kinds of people is the fact that they are very difficult to handle because of their resistance to change – especially growth and expansion.

The real problem is that they feel that the person who has just joined the workplace is out to get "their" job. At first, they did not need any help, and now, they still think that they don't need any help whatsoever. It does not matter how competent the other person is because the control freak will not welcome any ideas or suggestions that are not theirs.

To deal with such a person; what you need to do is get rid of turf wars by ensuring that you engage them fully during role allocation. Allow them to create their projects so that they feel as though they have a sense of tenure. If it is possible, you can separate their duties from those of other employees. Once they see that their roles are highly valuable to the company, they will ease off on their controlling attitude – giving the others ample space and time to go about their duties with minimal interruptions.

Stroke their ego

According to research, there is evidence that shows control freaks are often very insecure. The thing with such people is that they often fight just so that they can retain control, considering that they are not sure of themselves. Such people hate trying new things and desperately are afraid of new situations and events. They feel that by retaining control over their work surrounding – something familiar to them – they can keep their insecurities in check.

Well, unfortunately, the approach they use in controlling things and people around them depicts their domineering and overbearing attitudes. This is precisely what stands to undermine their self-esteem and confidence further – especially if they spent the time to evaluate their behaviors honestly.

To deal with such kind of people, you need to find a way to help them regain their control so that they can feel secure. The best way to do this is for you to appeal to their ego. While they may come off as confident people, the truth is that inside, they are fragile. They are just hiding under that assertive shell so that they can win others' approval. Before they can offer you any help, go to them and ask them to help you with a difficult task. Even when you feel as though things are not looking up, simply compliment them on anything so that they can relax and make it easier for them to relinquish control over small things.

Stand your ground

There are instances when you feel that there is nothing you can do to appease someone who is controlling. This is because they firmly believe that they know best. They will even go as far as throwing tantrums if they don't get their way.

The best way to handle them is to try and assess what it is that you disagree on. If it is something important, you should stand your ground. While this may stir up conflict and friction at the workplace, it will help them know that not everyone can toy around. The trick is that you choose your battles with caution. If it is an issue of how the office should be cleaned, ask yourself whether it is something you would want to die for.

Take note of the little things

Just like stroking their ego, taking note of small things is about paying attention to what their needs are. Whatever it is, ensure that you pay attention to these tendencies. Reassure them that they are doing an incredible job. Tell them that the place would not be as excellent as it is without them. Praise them for their underlying qualities, and before long, you will realize that their controlling attitude reduces significantly as they soak in praise!

Give a little

Is there someone in your office or home that thinks they know so much more than anyone else? Does it even matter that they believe this? Well, the truth is that in the grand scheme of things, the question that truly matters is if this person is involved in all your daily activities and your ability to do your job. If they don't stand in the way of you getting your job done, the best way to tame them would be to give to her selfish and immature attitude – and simply move on.

Ask questions

One thing you will note about a control freak is that they often are obnoxious. Several people around them dismiss them because of their bossy attitude and desire to control every little thing. Well, the truth is that in reality, they just desire to be part of something – and can offer valuable input – if only people would listen.

Therefore, the next time you encounter a control freak at home or in the office, and they want to boss you around, ask them pointed questions about how they want this or that to be done. If they insist on installing the lights in a specific manner, ask them why they think it cannot be done differently. It could be that they have a phobia for heights, and that is why they insist that it be done a different way than that avoids falling. This allows you to realize that these control issues do not hurt and have the potential of affecting their security in the workplace or at home.

If they are adamant that stationeries go to the right side of their desk and then picture frames on the left, demand for an explanation, there are times when you will realize that they don't have a valid reason for that. If it is not their desk, then that is unacceptable. However, if it is their desk, the best thing is for you to oblige. The point is for you to help them confront their obsessions so that you can know whether there is an actual control issue going on or there is something else subtler that goes beyond stationeries.

Spending time with them talking about these issues will help both of you resolve the problems amicably so that you can both get back to what matters and be productive at it.

If necessary, enlist the help

What if you are not able to reach a point of compromise with someone who is a control freak? In such a case, you can seek advice from your superiors or line manager. You must try to explain to them that your intention is not to cause disharmony in the office. Instead, what you are interested in is creating an atmosphere where each one of you can thrive.

This will also go a long way in helping the boss understand that you are not there to complain but that you have the company's best interest at heart. You must tell your manager that the other person's tendencies are getting in the way of you working and reaching your goals. Ask them to clarify what your roles and responsibilities are at the office. There is a chance that the management has no idea of what the situation is like, and asking them to step in will help a great deal to clear things up.

It is also essential that you are always ready to offer possible solutions to the issue so that your bosses are aware that you are also a team player. While working with someone who is controlling can be difficult, realize that it does not have to be impossible! Just a little effort aimed at understanding their motivations and alleviating their insecurities will go a long way in helping you work together in harmony.

Narcissists

Narcissists are people who are ready challenging to work mainly because of their big ego and vanity. The problem with them is that they pretend to know it all. If you have such a person at home or the workplace, you must determine where they are real experts and where they are pretentious.

If they are real experts, then your research should prove that they are knowledgeable in that area because of the validity of their ideas and information. You must not subjugate their ideas or permit any condescension. The trick is for you to be respectful when dealing with them. Where you feel they are wrong, simply correct them without being confrontational or overly aggressive.

Gossips

With the advent of technological devices, gossiping is no longer restricted to the water cooler. Today, people gossip with ease of emails and social media platforms. What is interesting is that in spite of all these technological innovations, chatting today at the office or home can be traced back to one single individual who always knows and shares information – whether true or false.

If you have such a person in your life, the best way to deal with them is to avoid sharing information with them or someone close to them. You must practice remaining cordial when around them. Whenever they try to pry into your life or that of others, gently pull away from the conversation and change the subject into something more productive and useful.

Bullies

These people are a fact of life, and the most unfortunate thing is that by the time they are graduating high school, if they will not have changed, then chances are that they will never change. These are the kind of people who end up taking their insecurities to the workplace, marriages, and friendships. The problem is thinking of others as weak and susceptible and hence use that to be vindictive. They will always try to get other people to gang up against one or more people around them.

When you are dealing with such a person, you must try as much as you can to hide your weaknesses. Stand up to them, and don't tolerate them being respectful to you. Don't get me wrong; I don't mean that you get aggressive with them. However, you must not allow them to interfere with your life. If they try to bring their attitude to your place of work or home, simply ask them to leave.

Slackers

These are the kind of people who are not motivated and are unreliable. They are the kind that cannot carry their weight. If you have never worked with one of these, thank you, God! They are the kind of people who will leave all the work to you. When you are asked to partner with them, ensure that the job assigned to them is done to completion. If not, then you should be prepared to take on their portion of work.

Trust me; they are out there to let people down – beware!

Pessimists

Some people view the world through shades of gray. They are the pessimists whose primary agenda is to dismiss every idea someone comes up with without necessarily offering an alternative. Much of their time is spent complaining about this or that. If you have such a person in your team, the trick is to remain positive. Remind them that you cannot just sit and do nothing; instead, they should give their contributions as well.

Oh, and be prepared to shoulder much of the work!

The hostile or bossy

The one thing I have learned when dealing with these kinds of people is that strength and tact goes a long way. People who feel as though they have been wronged tend to be violent.

The other trick is for you to try as much as you can to help them meet their needs without necessarily being aggressive or discriminatory about it. Try to stay away from any interaction with them that stirs up intense emotions like violence – as they say, don't hang out with the enemy when they are carrying a weapon or drinking! Check your actions to ensure that they don't stir up anger. In short, try not to be a pushover.

The worst thing you can do is strongly retaliate against an aggressive person. Remember that hostility often begets hostility. The best thing you can do is try to divert their attention to something more meaningful. This way, their anger tends to go down. Try to explain to them more about the situation pointing out common interests so that they are open to calm and rational ways of resolving the issue at hand.

The chronic complainer

These are the kind of people who will always find fault in everything you do. They will go to the extent of blaming you. They pretend as though they know all that should be done when, in fact, they are never open to correcting the situation themselves in the first place.

If you want to cope with these kinds of people, the first thing is for you to pay attention to all they have to say and then ask questions to seek clarification – even though you have been falsely accused or are guilty. The secret is for you not to complain, apologize, or be overly-defensive. If you do, then you are causing them to restate their concerns in a more heated manner. You must be severe and supportive of it. Accept the facts and get all the complaints in writing. Involve them in the process so that you all actively find the solution. Rather than dwelling too much on what is wrong, try to get them to think of what should be done.

The Super-Agreeable

Has anyone ever agreed with everything and anything you say to the point that they make you angry? Well, these are the super-agreeable people. While it is a good thing to get along with people at home and the workplace, some people agree with every idea you give, and then when things suddenly go south; they back down.

What you need to note about these people is that they are after approval. We all come from different family backgrounds with diverse upbringings. Some learned that the best way to get love is through pretense. In the same way, those people who are super-agreeable tend to promise heaven on earth but cannot deliver that. They will tell you, "I will submit the report tomorrow, or I will help you run errands." Don't be fooled; all they are doing is buttering you up.

The best way to handle them is to assure them that it is okay to say "No" when they feel like they will not be able to deliver. It is okay to speak the truth even when it is hard to spit it out. You must take time to ask them to try and be candid so that they can find it easy to come out and be frank about anything. When you support them overcome this habit, they will stop making promises they know they couldn't possibly keep. Show them that you value the relationship you have, and the truth won't hurt. Ensure that you let them know you are ready to compromise, considering that they will be fair and just.

Critics

Criticism is not all that bad, but the truth is that there are times and places for it. Debates are where the most effective solutions are birth. This is where some of the best minds challenge every point of view in the room.

But is that always the case with criticism? Are there demanding critics?

Indeed, there are so many demanding critics whose criticism is destructive. They are not seeking answers. They are not even concerned with the give and take that leads to a strong team and a consensus. They are the people who behave like politicians. I like to think of critics as spectators and not players.

Look around your office; is there is a critic there? Is your spouse or friend a critic?

Often, you will notice that critics are the kind of people who will always be quick to point a finger, and yet when their help is needed, they will not lift one. They are the kind of people who will not cooperate within the project, and it is their negative attitude that makes it hard to work and achieve the set goals in a team.

Chapter 3: Resolving Conflicts

Jeanette and Charles are biologists. They were chosen to work on a research project together. Right from the start, Jeanette decided her colleague was morose, and didn't have the qualities necessary to work effectively as part of a team, on a demanding project.

After two weeks, Jeanette was at the end of her rope. Not only was Charles as socially inept as a block of wood, he also refused to share his scientific data with her. The atmosphere in the small lab, where they spent entire days together, became unbearable. Jeanette found it harder and harder to sleep, and her work began to suffer. She broke out in pimples, although she'd never had acne in her life before. The dermatologist she consulted immediately concluded that her skin disorder was the result of stress.

Finally, after an out and out argument with Charles, Jeanette decided to get to the bottom of things. She discreetly questioned other colleagues who knew Charles, and tried to find out about his past behavior. And each time he became negative with her, she made sure to write down the circumstances that provoked the conflict.

This is a question Jeanette asked herself, once she discovered the underlying causes behind Charles' negative behavior, and was able to identify her own role in the situation.

If you find yourself facing a person who, like Charles, has been embittered by the vicissitudes of life - personal disappointments, frustrated ambitions, professional conflicts, etc. - it is possible to overcome the barrier between you without damaging either the other person or yourself, and at the same time assert yourself to advantage.

Here's what to do:

- Ask for a meeting with the other person. If necessary, set a definite time and place. Try to make sure you won't be interrupted, and show the other person that you take the problem seriously.

- Start the discussion by stating that you believe the situation between you isn't clear. Something's definitely wrong.
- Wait for the person's reaction.
- Depending on the way the person reacts - or doesn't react - to your overtures, determine what type of "difficult" person you're dealing with.
- Be diplomatic! For example, after Jeanette set up a meeting with Charles, she didn't come right out and say, "Oh, I know all about what happened with your job transfer, and about your insecurity because you didn't go to a great school!"

Above all, don't be condescending or arrogant. And finally, something we can't seem to repeat often enough - DON'T TRY TO READ THE OTHER PERSON'S MIND. There's nothing more exasperating. How would you feel if someone was constantly doing it to you?

Example:

Here's how Jeanette got the conversation rolling:

"I feel there's some tension between us, and it's beginning to affect our work. I don't have as much experience as you do, and I was hoping to learn, a lot and improve my methods by working with you. But that's not happening. Do you think we're just incompatible? Is it the mistakes I've made that are bothering you? Is it the methods I use? I'd like to know what you think about it."

Stop trying to change other people

This is probably one of the most important keys to success in the area of human relations. We seem to possess an extraordinary capacity for creating illusions about the people around us, and especially about those we love. We often love people despite their faults, but only because we hope that someday they'll change and conform more closely to our desired image of them.

We spend years trying to get someone to change the way we want them to, until the day comes when we realise that changing another person is beyond our powers, especially if the change we are striving to produce runs counter to that person's own will.

When that day comes, we either start loving the person for who s/he is, or we stop loving them altogether - and that's where the danger lies.

Human beings can change

This is not to deny that people have the capacity to change.

It is evident that every human being evolves throughout the course of his / her existence. The environment causes us to change, as does the exercise of individual will, and this continues right up to very old age.

But it is during the first twelve years of life that people are most malleable. And yet, even during this first phase of existence, we have the utmost difficulty getting our children to conform to our wishes.

It goes without saying that once a person reaches adulthood, his / her evolution is almost completely beyond the conscious control of anyone else, under normal circumstances.

Try to remember the last time you had an unpleasant or painful encounter with someone, and said to yourself, "If only he were less uptight!" or "If only he were a little more tolerant…" or "If only old people were less demanding…" or "If only my kids were less selfish…" and so on.

Our wishes are not reality

Our error consists of believing that others should conform to our desires, and when they don't live up to our expectations, we blame them for it. We label them difficult or intolerant, selfish or overly demanding, indecisive or vain, etc.

The important thing is to realise that we're dealing with a real human being, and that every person has his/her qualities and faults. Other people are not projections of our imagination - we can't eliminate aspects of their personality that do not live up to our expectations, nor can we give them qualities we think they should possess.

That's why I'm so pleased whenever someone says, "You're disappointing me." To me, this means that the person hasn't been in touch with who I really am, but with a projection of who they think I am - in other words, with themselves. Imagine all the time we waste being a screen for other people's projections!

So the intelligent thing to do is obviously to become conscious of the reality of people around us, both of those who please us, and those who don't. We should also know that we can contribute significantly to their happiness and self fulfilment, on condition that they wish us to do so.

You can influence people's attitudes

While you may do your utmost to improve a situation between yourself and a "difficult" person, you should under no circumstances attempt to modify that person's personality. You will not succeed, and in any case it won't be of any use.

The only thing you can do is modify a person's attitude toward you. It is towards this goal that you should direct all your efforts.

You do more for the person this way than by trying to change his / her personality, and make the person easier to live with, from your point of view, of course.

By bringing the problem or conflict that is poisoning your relationship out in the open, you help the other person see him / herself more clearly, just as you've been able to see yourself better because of the efforts you've been making.

And it is by becoming aware of the forces, the ambitions, the desires and repulsions that make us act in certain ways, that enable us to take control of our lives, assert ourselves and attain fulfilment.

Distance yourself

When faced with a difficult relationship, we tend to get deeply involved. We lose all sense of objectivity. Our day to day lives are soon affected, as we become preoccupied with the problem. We may even become obsessed by the difficult person in question, and the problems s/he is causing.

This is what happened at first to Jeaneatte, our biologist. Overwhelmed by her problems with Charles, she became unable to sleep, couldn't do her work properly, until she took hold of herself and analysed the situation as if she were an outside observer.

But keeping your distance from someone who exerts a strong influence is easier said than done. Difficult people seem to know how to trigger negative emotions - they always seem to know just what to say or do to make us upset.

Adopt a strategy and apply it

In your exchanges with difficult people, there are really only two types of strategy to choose from. Either you get involved in a power struggle, with the aim of coming out on top. Or you look for a way to achieve satisfying results while taking the other person's needs into account.

The upper hand

As we've seen in section before, there are different types of "difficult" people, so it follows that our strategy will depend on the type of attack that you are subjected to.

For example, if you're dealing with a negative type, who gradually manages to intoxicate your mind with measured doses of pessimism, you'd be less inclined to get into a power struggle situation than if you were dealing with a "steamroller" type.

When we look at the world around us, we see that the struggle for survival seems to resemble a frantic competition, where the big fish swallow up the little fish, and the strong dominate the weak. So there's a great temptation to consider our relations with difficult people as a struggle, where the only aim is to gain the upper hand.

However, you've probably noticed that in the preceding parts we have avoided suggesting that gaining the upper hand become the main objective of your training in interpers on al relations.

Avoid win - lose situations

The reason for this approach is that wherever you have a win - lose situation, the loser will not rest until s/he has found some way of getting revenge. We could even qualify this reaction as "natural" since it is so common.

But if you think about it, you'll see that although the animal kingdom does rely on the balance created by the strong devouring the weak, nowhere in nature do we see a weak animal waiting patiently for years, and sometimes even for generations if necessary, in order to reverse the roles and exact revenge on another animal, for a past humiliation.

This is a characteristically human trait, which, as we know, results in all kinds of disasters - wars, famine, repression, needless destruction, and so on.

This is why our recommendations are aimed at "restoring communication at the point where it broke down" and "defining your position, as well as that of the other person, if necessary." Not letting someone walk all over you doesn't necessarily mean dominating that person. It means not letting another person dominate you and, based on this affirmation of self, doing something constructive about the situation.

Win-win strategy and the game of life

Another way to approach our relations with others is to try to produce a situation that satisfies both our needs, as well as the other person's.

There are people for whom we feel no special sympathy, who surprise us with the generous and unsolicited things they do for us. Each time we feel like a winner in our relations with them, we are, consciously or unconsciously, scoring a golden point in their favour. The day may come when they do something that tips the scales, this time in a positive sense, and we find ourselves experiencing an immense feeling of gratitude towards them.

A narrow view of life could give us the impression that nature is nothing more than a huge battlefield. But science has shown us that, above all, nature is a study in balance. If a species disappears because of a predator's success, the predator will also disappear, for lack of food.

The more progress we make in understanding the universe, the more we discover that everything is somehow related to everything else. Winning by forcing someone else to lose out ultimately means setting yourself up to lose out as well. That's the way the game of life works. We're all in the same boat, and if I make a hole in the hull because I want you to sink, I'm eventually going to sink too.

In fact, what is occurring now, thanks to developments in science and communication, is a mutation of consciousness which is unprecedented in the history of humanity. We are discovering that the choice of being a winner by making others losers, is not a real choice at all. The real choice is that either we both win together, or we both lose together. This is the only alternative we have. And that's why we must develop a win - win attitude, to the point where it becomes a reflex, in almost all situations.

When we're dealing with likable, nice, easy-going people, it happens naturally. We find certain people "disarming" and couldn't imagine doing anything to harm them, probably because we'd feel too guilty afterwards.

On the other hand, when we have to deal with difficult persons, things become a lot harder, probably because we feel they have wronged us in some way, and we wish to punish them for it.

We have the choice

However, even in these types of situations we have the choice of creating a relationship based on force and domination, a relationship which is bound to fail eventually, or to look for a way to satisfy both parties.

When faced with a difficult person, you have to be very clear on what strategy you intend using: are you going to try and crush the other person in order to experience the pleasure (albeit very temporary) of victory or revenge, without thinking about the price you'll have to pay later for your elation?

Or are you going to protect yourself first, and then look for ways to establish a constructive dialogue?

These two fundamental options are always available to you. The only variable, therefore, is your choice of approach.

Become aware of negative interaction

The main problem with applying a win - win approach is that the negativity which characterises the communication can easily engender more negativity in you. This is what is meant by negative interaction - the old vicious circle.

They're sometimes impossible to avoid. We're so upset and exasperated that any possibility of improving the situation, or bringing it to a positive conclusion, seems very remote.

When you're the target of anger, slander, and injustice, it can be all but impossible to control yourself, and not react in kind.

However, if you wish to assert yourself, improve the situation, and help the other person all at the same time, then you have no choice. You must learn to control the way you react, in order to break the vicious circle and set up a cycle of positive interaction in its place.

What you're being asked to do, in order to defuse conflict situations and start communicating with difficult persons, is to respond to their anger with patience, to their disdain with respect, and to their harmful intentions with benevolence.

If you think that this is a superhuman task, reserved for angels and saints, then you will inevitably perpetuate the cycles of misunderstanding and violence you encounter. But rest assured, although reacting in this way may be reserved for "evolved" persons, it is by no means beyond the reach of the average human being.

The simple fact that you've read this far is sufficient proof that developing such reflexes would not present much of a problem for you. All you have to do is practice the exercises suggested a little later on.

Above all, strive for positive interaction

Here's some good news: in the same way that negative attracts negative, positive attracts positive. The hard thing to do is reverse the current, and we'll be looking here at a few methods for effecting this change.

We've already stressed the importance of not responding to aggression with aggression. We must refer to it again, since it is the cornerstone of achieving any significant changes in your conflicting or difficult relationships.

We analysed how difficult persons seem to have the capacity for bringing out the worst in us, for bringing us down to their level, so that we find ourselves doing the very same things we've been criticising them for doing! However, don't forget that as difficult as a person may be, s/he is still capable of responding positively to the right kind of stimulus; everyone (almost) possesses all the necessary resources for becoming an open, positive and communicative person.

To start the process, you must first categorically refuse to participate in any destructive games. Then, when attempts to involve you in such games cease, you can start your work being the engine that pulls the relationship in a positive direction.

Get rid of all the garbage and junk that is weighing you down. Start collecting "golden points" in all your relationships. Create conditions for positive interaction, for "virtuous" circles instead of vicious ones. I guarantee your life will undergo a miraculous change for the better.

Chapter 4: Effective Phrases that Can Be Used

Have you dealt with someone who seems so unreasonable that you ask, "Hey, what's up with that guy?" In this chapter we're going to take a look at how people like Mr. Potter and Patti's mom are wired and what makes them tick. Then we'll examine how to accurately assess the unreasonable person so we can deal with him or her effectively. Conflict with unreasonable people goes well only when we first know and understand what we're up against.

Unreasonable People Are Everywhere

Unreasonable people are called many things. Several of the terms contain swear words, refer to body parts, or deliberately insult the person's ancestry. We've all heard them, and most of us have used them on occasion. The list that follows is by no means exhaustive but includes some of the common terms, omitting the more tasteless ones.

big baby	loon	prima donna
bull in a china shop	loony bird	psycho

bully	loser	schmuck
control freak	martyr	smooth operator
crazy-maker	messiah	snake in the grass
creep	moron	turkey
drama queen	nut	victim
freak show	nut case	wacko
guilt tripper	pain in the neck	weasel
horse's tail	personality disorder	wolf in sheep's clothing
jerk	piece of work	

If unreasonable people are despotic rulers of nations, we call them "mad men." In the Bible, they are called "fools" or "the wicked." Unfortunately, we encounter unreasonable people throughout life. They first show up as toddlers throwing temper tantrums. At that point, the unreasonable person is a kid who needs to mature—to develop better ways of handling frustration.

The ones who don't mature (for various reasons) show up again in elementary school as bullies on the playground. Again, the need is to grow—to learn more mature ways of dealing with peers. Those who fail to mature become adults who are called the names just mentioned. The unreasonable person is a child in an adult's body, a person who needs to grow up—to learn more mature ways of handling relationships and conflict.

Unreasonable people truly are everywhere, and a large percentage of the population meets the criteria we'll be discussing. We run into them at work, at school, at church, in the community, at the doctor's office, in government, in entertainment, at family gatherings, and in marriages. In fact, there are sleeper cells of unreasonable people all over the place. The following descriptive phrases are commonly used in reference to unreasonable people:

arrogant	going mental	repugnant
audacious	high maintenance	self-important
complex	high schoolish	sick
confusing	insecure	slimy
crazy	insufferable	stubborn

crazy as a loon	irritating	toxic
difficult	loony	treacherous
disordered	manipulative	two-faced
ego-centric	narcissistic	wacked
full of it	psychotic	

Joyce Landorf Heatherly referred to unreasonable people as "irregular."[1] Susan Forward refers to them as "emotional blackmailers."[2] Henry Cloud and John Townsend call them "unsafe."[3] Scott Peck refers to them as "evil."[4] Sometimes the word "political" is used, usually in a pejorative sense, communicating the idea that the people are two-faced, back-biting, power-hungry, self-advancing, conniving, and duplicitous. Hence, someone will say, "I didn't want to be on that board because it's so political." Jimmy Stewart, who played the title character in another Frank Capra film, *Mr. Smith Goes to Washington,* encountered the worst form of politics when he arrived in the nation's capital. Patriotism had attracted him to the nobility of public service, but he was depressingly disillusioned after discovering that some of his most idealized heroes were drastically different people in private than what they appeared to be in public—one of the chief characteristics of unreasonable people.

We are simultaneously fascinated by and frustrated with unreasonable people. We make movies about them, write books about them, and keep up with them through the tabloids. They are often people with dazzling positives alongside glaring negatives, and it's that mix of opposing traits that makes them so interesting and confounding. We often make one or more of the following statements about an unreasonable person:

He has some screws loose.

She thinks the world revolves around her.

She'll stab you in the back.

He creeps me out.

She wears me out.

There's one in every crowd.

She's never wrong about anything.

When she fights, she shows her true colors.

He gives me the heebie jeebies.

Here comes Joe, hide!

Once you're on her bad side, you can't get back.

He's always got an angle.

She thinks everyone's out to get her.

She sucks all the air out of the room.

He thinks the rules don't apply to him.

Being around her is a real soap opera.

Joe's wife has got to be a saint.

Unreasonable People Haven't Grown Up

The house I grew up in was next to a neighborhood park, and one of my playmates, Hector, lived across the field. He and I would play in the park with other kids from the neighborhood. Several things stand out in my memories about Hector. First, I had never known anyone else with that name. Second, he always wore the same pair of dirty, untied tennis shoes. Third, he drooled a lot and wiped it with a handkerchief his mom had given him. Finally, he was always smiling, and we had lots of fun.

This story probably makes you feel good if it conjures up pleasant memories from your own childhood. But I left out an important piece of information. Hector was in his twenties back then. He had a condition that left him mentally and physically impaired. His shoes were untied because he couldn't tie them. He drooled because he was unable to control his saliva. He was happy playing with little children because his own mental development had stalled at the level of a small child.

Now how do you feel about the story? Hector, it turns out, was chronologically old but developmentally young. It's tragic when a discrepancy exists between the two.

Unreasonable people have that sort of discrepancy. While it's true that everyone has maturity gaps, unreasonable people have pervasive impairments in their abilities to handle people problems. Some of the parts that are needed to flex and adjust in conflict situations didn't develop along with the rest of the parts, leaving them inflexible and rigid, lacking the "give and take" possessed by reasonable people. They are grown-ups who haven't grown up.

Why They Stopped Growing

Frequently a reasonable person being driven crazy by an unreasonable person will ask me, "What do you think is wrong with him?" That's hard to say. The problem could have an internal cause, such as something genetic or a brain malfunction that developed later in life (nature). Or it could have to do with external factors, such as having a deficient upbringing (nurture). Or it could be the result of his choices (what he's done with nature and nurture). Often it's a combination of factors. For whatever reason, the unreasonable person passed up or missed opportunities to grow up, becoming chronologically older while remaining developmentally young. He or she is now a child in a grown-up's body.

What Stopped Growing

Reasonable people have these muscles, which become stronger with use. If two reasonable people argue and handle their flaws well, they are likely to reach a resolution. Unreasonable people don't have some or all of these muscles. They never developed them, or they've become atrophied from years of disuse.

Unreasonable people have an aversion to personal wrongness that extends far beyond anything experienced by reasonable people. To them, being wrong presents a threat to survival that equals most physical threats. Unreasonable people put all of their energy into safeguarding rightness—to staying safe—and none into solving conflict problems. They're not interested in solving problems if doing so requires the acknowledgment of wrongness.

Let's look at the five "reason muscles" and what they look like in unreasonable people. Remember, having these muscles and using them is what distinguishes a reasonable person from someone who is not.

The Humility Muscle

The first muscle needed to handle wrongness well is the *humility* muscle, which gives a person the ability to acknowledge potential personal wrongness. When reasonable people use this muscle, the stance is, "I could be wrong, you could be right, let's talk." Reasonable people, who have healthy humility muscles, can handle being wrong if being right requires sacrificing the truth. They believe, though perhaps reluctantly, in the maxim, "Truth is your best ally." It may be painful to acknowledge wrongness, but they'll do so because being truthful has a higher value to them than being right.

Unwilling to allow for the possibility of wrongness, unreasonable people will sacrifice truth if being truthful means being wrong. They'll even lie to avoid being wrong. In fact, some unreasonable people revise truth so routinely that they delude themselves and come to believe their own revisions. The stance taken is, "I'm right, you're wrong, end of discussion." They can be arrogant and inflexible. That's why you can't reason with them. Your attempts at reasonableness won't work because they're not interested in reason; they're only interested in winning or in being right.

The Awareness Muscle

The second muscle needed is the *awareness* muscle, which enables us to observe areas of actual personal wrongness. Having this muscle, the reasonable person's stance is, "I see where I'm wrong." They see their strengths but also understand their weaknesses. Unreasonable people have ruled out the possibility of wrongness, so the stance taken is, "I only see where I'm right." Unreasonable people are notoriously lacking in self-awareness, not seeing the flaws in themselves that others so clearly see. Therefore, when problems occur, they automatically assume that others caused them.

The press box is the part of our personalities that enables us to make big-picture self-observations. For unreasonable people, the wires connecting the press box to the sidelines phones are severed. They don't have press box conversations and are sorely lacking in awareness. That's why we say:

She has no idea how she comes across.

He's a bull in a china shop.

He's clueless about the part he played in that argument.

Her husband sees it, her kids see it, her boss sees it. Everybody sees it but her.

She's oblivious.

Relationships are like mirrors in which we catch glimpses of the good and bad parts of ourselves. Reasonable people make use of the feedback that relationships provide. But unreasonable people catch no reflections of their flaws in relational mirrors.

The Responsibility Muscle

Sometimes referred to as a conscience, the *responsibility* muscle enables us to be bothered by personal wrongness. Unreasonable people are weak in the conscience department. While the reasonable person observes personal faults and cringes, the unreasonable person shrugs when flaws are pointed out. His or her stance is, "If I'm wrong, so what?"

One Sunday afternoon I sat riveted to a documentary about a well-known American who was great in public but not so great in private. With the passage of time, his once-concealed infidelities have become part of the historical record. A family friend was interviewed who recounted a conversation in which she asked him why he would take such chances and jeopardize his legacy. In response he calmly replied, "I guess I just can't help it." She then made this astute observation:

He always lived his life in compartments. There was the public compartment, in which he accomplished these great things, all of which were true. But he also had an unseen compartment in which he was repeatedly unfaithful to his wife and children. I think he knew there were discrepancies between the compartments, but they just didn't bother him that much.

In effect, the unreasonable person looks in the mirror, sees the glob of spinach on his teeth, doesn't like what he sees, and decides to quit looking in mirrors. The reasonable person *seeks* out truth to change for the better. The unreasonable person *runs* from truth to avoid discomfort.

The Empathy Muscle

The fourth muscle needed is the *empathy* muscle. Empathy is the ability to be bothered if our personal wrongness hurts others. It enables us to understand the effects we have on the other person and to use that understanding to govern our words and actions.

When a reasonable person uses this muscle, the resulting stance is, "It bothers me when my wrongness hurts you." He allows that understanding to shape how he behaves toward others. The unreasonable person is empathy deficient. His stance is, "I'm only bothered when your wrongness hurts me." Consequently, the unreasonable person is often described as "cruel" or "insensitive" in his dealings with others. That's why we say, "It's all about him" or "I can't believe she could say (or do) that" or "Watch out, he'll stab you in the back." The unreasonable person gives little consideration to the impact of his words and actions on others. Reciprocal empathy is a realistic expectation in conflict with reasonable people. With unreasonable people, however, we should anticipate self-serving motivation and behaviors.

The Reliability Muscle

The *reliability* muscle is the ability to correct personal wrongness. A reasonable person is bothered by his flaws and determines, "When I'm wrong, I'll change." Since the unreasonable person fails to see his flaws, he is neither bothered by them nor sees the need to correct them. Consequently, his stance is, "I'll not change because I'm not wrong."

Prof. Howard Hendricks notes that people have two types of needs: *real needs* and *felt needs*.5 A real need must be felt before we'll do anything about it. For instance, you could have cancer but not know it—an undetected but very real malady that needs attention. If your doctor diagnosed it, you'd become aware of the illness, feel the need, and seek treatment. Evaluation and diagnosis would transform your real need into a felt need. Unreasonable people have flaws but don't see them, so they do nothing to correct them. Frequently a client being driven crazy by an unreasonable person remarks, "He's the one who really needs to be in here getting help." That may be true, but no one seeks help without first realizing help is needed. The unreasonable person doesn't see that anything is wrong with him, so why should he seek help? Change presupposes awareness.

That's why the Mr. Potters of the world rarely come to offices like mine—they believe there's nothing wrong with them. In *It's a Wonderful Life,* Mr. Potter saw himself as the good guy, the smart and powerful person looking after lazy and uneducated townsfolk. Having that view of himself, why would he ever change anything?

So here's what we're up against when we have conflict with unreasonable people. They automatically assume we're the ones in the wrong, they fail to see their contributions to the conflict, they claim no responsibility for any part of the problem, they're not bothered by the impact of their words and actions on us, and they change nothing because nothing about them needs changing. Is it any wonder that unreasonable people are so difficult for us to handle?

This chart summarizes the different outcomes when the "reason muscles" are used by reasonable people and not used by unreasonable people.

Outcomes of Reason Muscle Use

Reason Muscle	When Used (Reasonable People)	When Not Used (Unreasonable People)
Humility	I could be wrong, you could be right, let's talk	I'm right, you're wrong, end of discussion
Awareness	I see where I'm wrong	I only see where I'm right
Responsibility	It bothers me when I'm wrong	If I'm wrong, so what?
Empathy	It bothers me when my wrongness hurts you	I'm only bothered when your wrongness hurts me
Reliability	When I'm wrong, I'll change	I'll not change because I'm not wrong

The Unreasonable Person's Conflict Goal

When two reasonable people argue, their buttons get pushed, they react, they push buttons, they fail to use their "reason muscles," they make mistakes, and it may look and sound pretty ugly. But ultimately they are heading for the same objective: solving the problem. When a reasonable person argues with an unreasonable person, they have different objectives. The reasonable person's conflict goal is resolution while the unreasonable person's goal is rightness.

My two oldest children are girls born three years apart. They are both now extremely articulate, but when the youngest was first learning to talk, she was consistently out chattered by her loquacious older sister. Realizing her verbal disadvantage, the youngest would start swinging her fists. She hoped to accomplish physically what couldn't be accomplished verbally.

Similarly, an unreasonable person in conflict with a reasonable person is at a disadvantage because he's fighting someone who has something he doesn't possess—"reason muscles." He lacks what's necessary to do the right things with the wrongness. Therefore, he opts for a different conflict goal—rightness—which requires no wrongness acknowledgment. When the dust settles, he doesn't care about mutually satisfying problem solutions, but he does care about being right. To the unreasonable person, being right is entwined with his identity as a person and/or survival.[6] He needs to eat, he needs to breathe, and he needs to be right.

The Unreasonable Person's Means of Reaching the Goal: Drama

Unable and/or unwilling to tolerate wrongness, the unreasonable person opts for the only acceptable conflict outcome to him or her—rightness—and the method used to achieve that outcome is usually *drama*.[7] For example, suppose you're in a checkout line and the lady in front of you has two-year-old Suzie in her shopping cart. Suzie begs for something off the rack close to the register, and mom says no. Suzie asks again. Mom says no again. Suzie begs louder. Mom says no louder. Customers six aisles away have now joined you as members of the audience. The power struggle escalates to a crescendo until finally…guess what happens. Mom gives in. Suzie wins. Suzie's agitation drops considerably while Mom's agitation spikes through the stratosphere. Suzie is now the calm, good guy in control. Mom is now the exasperated bad guy who's out of control.

Lacking the maturity to reason, Suzie has just staged *a drama* to get what she wants and wins without using any "reason muscles." When toddlers do this, we call them spoiled brats. When adolescents do this, we call them bullies. When adults do this, we call them unreasonable people, jerks, and any of the myriad other names we come up with. In fact, dealing with an adult unreasonable person is very much like dealing with a child throwing a temper tantrum.

Some unreasonable people are openly dramatic, the kind we refer to as "drama queens" (or "drama kings") while others stage dramas in ways that are almost undetectable. Most unreasonable people missed attending Good Conflict Camp, but they all attended Drama School, where they developed into thespians of the highest order. That's why certain terms have become associated with unreasonable people: theatrics, grandstanding, mind games, soap operas.

I'm sometimes asked, "Do they know what they're doing? Do they plan out these dramas deliberately?" Good question. It's less likely that they plan them and more likely that drama has been used so routinely that it's done without conscious deliberation. Perhaps some people do both. Many unreasonable people seem to get so caught up in their drama that they lose the ability to distinguish between drama and real life.

Drama's Purpose

On March 4, 1933, Franklin Roosevelt was about to be inaugurated as president of the United States during one of the nation's most difficult periods, the Great Depression. In his thirties Roosevelt was stricken with polio, rendering his leg muscles useless. Having to rely exclusively on his arms, he developed enormous upper body strength. Leg braces, which could be locked into place, enabled him to stand upright when giving speeches.

Roosevelt knew the populace was demoralized and needed leadership that was strong, visionary, and courageous. He also understood that the picture of a president taking the oath of office from a wheelchair would not inspire confidence in a day when most people doubted the capabilities of disabled individuals. These images would be broadcast to a depressed nation using the newly developed media of the day—"talkies" or motion pictures with sound.

So Roosevelt devised a plan. After being discreetly helped from his chair, he used his powerful arms to brace himself on the arms of men on either side as they all made their way to the front. They had carefully choreographed, paced, and timed their movements in such a way that Roosevelt appeared to be walking with the group. In reality, his legs only lightly brushed the floor as he was carried along. His braces were locked into place at the podium, and he took the oath of office. To a beleaguered nation, he stood and delivered his inaugural address, which contained the confidence-inspiring line, "The only thing we have to fear is fear itself."

Here's my point. Roosevelt had atrophied muscles that were incapable of use and, had this knowledge been revealed, his leadership and survival as president would likely have been jeopardized. Therefore, he learned to act strong in places where he was actually weak. The strategy worked. And that's what the unreasonable person does. He has atrophied "reason muscles" and, if this were revealed, he'd have to admit wrongness, something he's unwilling to face because it threatens his survival. He uses drama to act strong where he is actually weak. Roosevelt performed his drama for a noble purpose—to provide strong national leadership. The unreasonable person performs his drama for self-serving reasons—to maintain rightness and avoid wrongness.

Chapter 5: Effective Attitude

Avoiding the Drama

Before we had children, Penny and I were talking with a wise couple about the familiar scene of kids throwing grocery store temper tantrums. They explained how they handled this situation with their own children, and we logged their idea for future reference, determined to employ the strategy should we ever need it. A few years later, Penny was in the checkout line and our little girl began begging relentlessly for a piece of junk on a rack nearby. Penny leaned over and said, "Begging is not allowed, and if you ask for it one more time, we'll go home." As expected, she begged again. Penny quietly picked her up, left the cart, and walked out of the store with our girl screaming her head off, conveying to shoppers that a kidnapping was in progress. Penny calmly strapped her into the car seat, drove home, and no other discipline followed. On the next grocery store trip, the begging started again. But this time Penny leaned over and said, "Now, I've told you that begging is not allowed. Remember what happened the last time?" That did it. No more begging. Displeasure, yes; begging, no.

What we see is a drama staged and a drama avoided. Our little girl staged the drama hoping to play the role of *master,* to be in charge. But remember, dramas only succeed if others play their parts. Penny avoided participation by neither giving in nor displaying aggravation—two different forms of participating. Therefore, the drama strategy failed and was not attempted the next time around. As good drama critics, let's review this play and make some post-drama observations.

- To handle this situation so well, Penny had to go against her grain. She was prone to get pulled into the power struggle, get upset, argue, threaten, or (worse yet) give in to keep the peace. She countered her natural reactions by opting, instead, for preplanned responses. *Drama avoidance requires planning.*
- The strategy cost her something—she had to go back to the store and shop again. But we had previously determined that the cost of reinforcing this undesirable pattern was higher than the time and energy it cost her to reshop. *Drama avoidance may cost something.*
- In this case, our plan succeeded on the first attempt, but Penny was prepared to repeat the strategy if needed until it did work. *Drama avoidance requires persistence.*
- The outcome of our plan had a good effect, in this case for both parties. Penny got to shop with less aggravation. Our girl was forced to grow up just a little bit that day, developing better ways of handling herself. *Drama avoidance brings about growth.*

Again, unreasonable people are children in the bodies of adults. They stage dramas not unlike the one just discussed, which succeed only if others participate. Participation provides a stage on which the unreasonable person's drama is performed. How can we avoid becoming drama participants? By avoiding three enticements: button pushes, reactions, and pushing buttons.

Avoiding Button Pushes

Unreasonable People Know Our Buttons

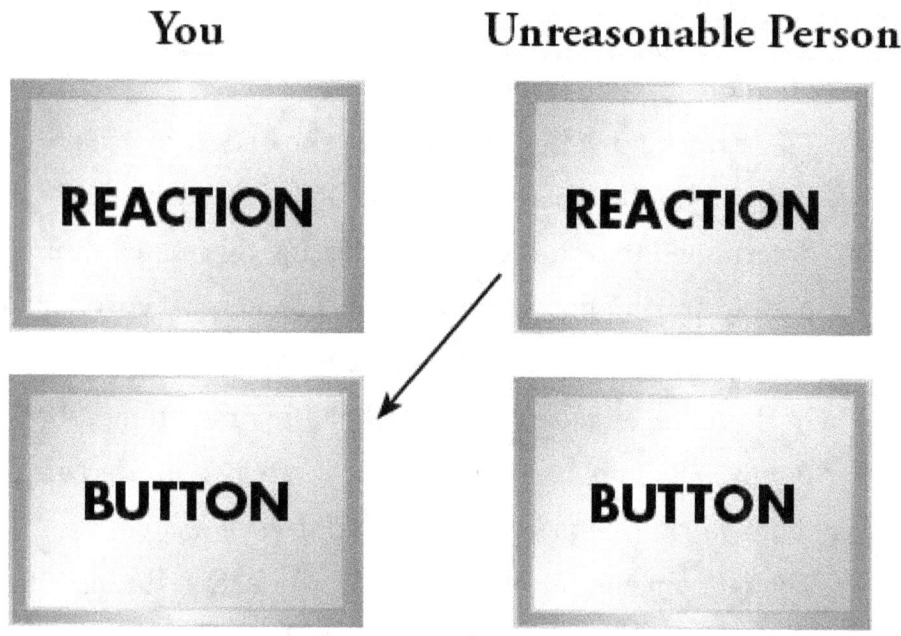

The unreasonable person pushes our buttons hoping for a reaction. He typically understands us better than we understand him. He or she knows where our buttons are and how to push them. Unreasonable people are good at enticing participation because drama success is perceived as necessary for their survival. Reasonable people are not naturally good at resisting enticements because that's not how we relate. Therefore, we must develop the skill.

Expect Attacks

The unreasonable person may push our buttons in predictably obvious ways or ambush us in unpredictably subtle ways.

Obvious Attacks

Examples of obvious attacks include insults, besmirching of character, slanderous accusations, name-calling, defamations, unjustified criticisms, and blatant lies. The unreasonable person taunts and eggs us on, hoping desperately for a knee-jerk reaction that places us squarely into the drama.

Subtle Attacks (Manipulations)

While obvious attacks are actively aggressive, subtle attacks are passively aggressive or manipulative. Our buttons get pushed, but we don't see the attacks coming. We get ambushed or sucker-punched. Let's look at four types of manipulations.

Exploitation of weaknesses. An invading army attacks at the weakest spot. Terrorists strike where their opponents are most vulnerable. Similarly, the unreasonable person sniffs out our weaknesses and attacks us there. We all have buttons—places of weakness, immaturity, and inadequacy. When life requires us to be strong in a weak area, an internal dialogue takes place. Some people use the word "tapes" to describe this self-talk, as in "When I took that job, all of my old inadequacy tapes started playing, telling me I couldn't do it." Others refer to the dialogue using terms such as "the voices," "the committee," or "the choir." One British writer described it using a phrase from wartime England: "the internal saboteur."[1] The unreasonable person, who wants to defeat us in conflict, studies our weaknesses and allies himself with our internal saboteurs. When certain buttons are pushed, the internal saboteurs spring into action, doing their best to remind us of our weakness and make us feel awful about ourselves. Like a voice-activated recorder, the sound of his voice on the outside activates the tapes on the inside. If we believe the tapes, we get sucked into the drama and the exploitation succeeds.

Suppose you are generous to a fault. You're a very giving person, but an old tape inside your head says, *You really could do more for people, you know. What's wrong with you? You're so selfish.* Suppose also that you have someone in your life like Patti's mom, a Level 2 martyr, whose stance is, "I can't make it without you to rescue me." She constantly demands assistance for problems she could easily fix herself. If you decline a request, she says, "That's fine. I'll do it myself. I thought you were here for me, but I guess I was wrong." Your internal saboteur springs into action saying, *She's right, you know. If you were a better person, you'd go out of your way to help her. What's wrong with you?* You've been guilt tripped, and to escape the guilt, you acquiesce to the demand. Your weakness has been exploited, and you've become a player in the drama, saving a martyr supposedly in need of rescue.

Presumptions. Most of us have been taught to believe the best of people and to give them the benefit of the doubt. While reasonable people deserve such courtesies, unreasonable people don't. As a kind gesture, we may offer a ride to a hitchhiker. If he's a good guy, no problem. If he's a crook, our kindness gets us robbed. If we give an unreasonable person the benefit of the doubt, he may very well presume upon our good graces and use it to his advantage—a subtle attack.

Role shifts. If an unreasonable person can't entice us into playing the required part, he may shift roles in hopes that, when the drama ends, he'll be back in his preferred role.[2] Here are some different forms of role shifting:

If the *master role* is preferred: A master needs us to submit. If we don't, he may shift into the *messiah role,* someone rescuing a person in need. He gives us something, but the gift has strings attached. At that point the giver is no longer a helper but a controller, the assistance being accompanied by an obligation to submit.

If the *messiah role* is preferred: A messiah is a sacrificial giver and needs us to be grateful recipients. If we aren't, she may slip into the *martyr role,* saying, "After all I've done for you, this is the kind of treatment I get? Thanks a lot." If it works, we'll allow her to resume the messiah role so we can escape the guilt trip discomfort.

If the *martyr role* is preferred: Martyrs are either saved by messiahs or persecuted by masters, the roles we must play for the martyr role to succeed. If we don't, she may become a *master* and strike at us, hoping we'll strike back. If we do strike back, she can once again assume the role of a martyr, a person who suffers at the hands of others: "I can't believe you would treat me this way."

If the *mute role* is preferred: A mute wants to be untroubled and needs us to pretend along with him that everything is just fine. If we refuse to participate in the pretense or enable the denial, he may assume the role of a *martyr:* "We could get on with our lives if you wouldn't keep bringing up all our problems. Can we please move on?"

These role requirements are button-pushing, boundary-violating drama enticements. There is pressure to perform our roles so that the other's role achieves the desired outcome—becoming the good guy. That's why it wears us out. We can't relax and just be ourselves.

Learn from Your Mistakes

Pickpockets can do their chosen profession because people aren't expecting their pockets to get picked. Remember, unreasonable people are good at enticements, but reasonable people are not naturally good at resisting enticements and can easily get caught off guard. We will make mistakes, and slip-ups are inevitable. But it's important to learn from our mistakes and avoid repeating them. Beating ourselves up about slip-ups doesn't help, but safeguarding ourselves against further enticements does. We should avoid situations in which mistakes are likely to happen and rehearse how to handle the situation should it happen again.

When Patti Avoided Button Pushes

Long before she came to see me, Patti used the term "subtly manipulative" to describe her mom. To casual observers, she was always the pleasant and productive Betty Crocker, but to Patti and Bill she was frequently a Bette Davis-type vixen. Patti learned she had to keep up her guard in this game of "emotional chess" between her family and "the vixen."

Patti's mom was quite adept at utilizing her arsenal of subtle weapons. Her daughter had a tender spot for people and animals in need and would go out of her way to provide assistance whenever she could. Understanding this, her mom would make her own needs apparent, taking on the demeanor of a wounded pet. These attempts to capitalize on Patti's bigheartedness usually worked. When they did, Patti felt angry and presumed upon one more time. Yes, her mom was manipulative, but Patti came to see that it was her responsibility to avoid manipulation. When she studied her own buttons and worked out a better response, it became much harder for her mom to push them.

Having to think this way about her mom left Patti with a bad taste in her mouth, reflected in statements such as, "I can't believe I have to be so guarded with my own mother. Isn't that terrible?" Actually, Patti wasn't being terrible, she was being wise. The guilt she felt for having negative feelings about her mom was unwarranted. Her bad feelings served a good purpose—to make her aware of boundary violations. She couldn't feel good about what her mother was doing, but she could make use of what she felt to move toward good conflict.

Avoid Reactions

Controlling your reaction when your button is pushed

You	Unreasonable Person

Rudyard Kipling must have known some cantankerous unreasonable people. He said, "If you can keep your head when all about you are losing theirs and blaming it on you..."[3] The unreasonable person desperately needs us to react, to lose our heads, so our reactions can be used as evidence that we're crazy and he or she is not.

Figuratively speaking, he takes "snapshots" of our reactions and uses those images to build the case—to himself and others—that we're bad and he's good. "Photo albums" displaying pictures of our bad behavior are eagerly shown around. Another way to think about this is that he has an emotional "remote control" for us. When he pushes our buttons and observes a reaction, he's gratified. But if he doesn't see a reaction, he's frustrated and will push the buttons more vigorously. To keep from reacting, we must plan our responses so we won't display any reaction, thus stopping the manipulation

Accepting the Limits

We've been discussing Patti, a person in conflict with an unreasonable person. Here's a similar story, only this conflict was not between individuals but between nations—the United States and the Soviet Union. In 1917, the Bolshevik Revolution occurred. The Russian monarchy was overthrown and replaced by a communist form of government. The new Union of Soviet Socialist Republics was founded upon Marxist principles, bringing radical changes to this vast country that stretched from Europe's border to the Pacific. Though allied against Hitler's Germany in World War II, the United States and the Soviet Union distrusted each other, with suspicions coming to a head in the years following the war. The development of Soviet nuclear capabilities in the late 1940s kept tensions escalated for the next several decades as the planet endured the ever-present potential of thermonuclear annihilation.

We've all struggled to handle conflicts with individual unreasonable people. But in many respects, the United States at this time had to contend with a giant, global unreasonable person in the form of the Soviet Union. This applied not so much to individual citizens but to the communist leadership controlling the apparatus of government.

First, they had unused "reason muscles." Their worldview and ideologically driven commitments led them to believe:

The wrongness must be on the side of the U.S.

We only see where we're right.

If we're wrong, so what?

We're only bothered if the wrongness of the U.S. hurts us.

We're not wrong, so there is nothing to correct.

They truly believed they were good and the U.S. was bad. They accused the U.S. of the very things that were true of them. So great was their commitment to rightness that they were willing to sacrifice truth to maintain it. The ends justified the means. They believed that lying or any other vice was a virtue if it advanced the cause of world communism.

Second, they were Level 3 (dangerous) unreasonable people. They responded to conflict by threatening to annihilate the U.S. or anyone who challenged them.

Third, they were *masters* who needed others to play a subservient role. Their "satellites" in Eastern Europe had no independence, and any moves toward self-determination were soundly squelched by military force.

Fourth, Western nations, particularly the United States, experienced the same effects as those produced by individual unreasonable people. The USSR government drove us crazy, made us sick, and wore us out. The situation drained huge portions of our national resources.

Bad conflict is what happens when we react to each other's reactions. Armed with atomic weapons that could be delivered atop intercontinental ballistic missiles (ICBMs), the two nations could ill-afford bad conflict reactions. One of these almost occurred in 1962 when the Soviets attempted to deploy offensive nuclear weapons on the island of Cuba, placing American population centers within striking distance of Soviet missiles. This was unacceptable to the U.S. and, for a few days, the world teetered on the precipice of nuclear war, in which an attack by either side would have led to retaliation by the other. In this case, the reactive cycle would have resulted in millions of deaths.

To avoid the horrific effects of bad conflict, the two nations became engaged in what was called the "Cold War," a conflict in which few shots were fired but tensions remained escalated. It wasn't a hot, shooting war due largely to the policy of "Mutually Assured Destruction" (MAD). That is, a nuclear first strike by either side would trigger a retaliatory response by the other, assuring the destruction of the initiator. Thus, the policy served to deter first strike impulses. "Peaceful coexistence" was the term used to describe the Cold War relationship of the two superpowers. While MAD helped to lower the potential of bad conflict, there was still the question about how to have good conflict with a giant, global unreasonable person. A vigorous debate developed among Westerners about how peace could best be achieved.

Generally there were two schools of thought. The first was the "peace through reason" approach. This view held that the Soviet leaders were reasonable people and wanted peace just like us; we simply misunderstood each other. The expectation, therefore, was that Western disarmament gestures would impress the Soviets and be reciprocated by their own disarmament gestures, making the world an increasingly safer place. The other school of thought was the "peace through strength" approach. This view held that the Soviet leaders were less interested in peace and more interested in winning, in achieving their global ideological objectives. Consequently, Western disarmament gestures would simply be exploited by the Soviets, giving them a position of nuclear superiority and making the world an even more dangerous place.

For many years the "peace through reason" approach was attempted, and the Soviets did in fact exploit it to gain the upper hand, leaving the prospects for peace even more elusive. Then, in the early 80s, we shifted strategies and began dealing with the

Soviets as global Level 3 masters who wanted to win. The "peace through strength" method was employed. The U.S. refused to play its designated role in the unreasonable person drama—subservience. We increased rather than decreased the strength of our military. For the Soviets, the expense of regaining and maintaining the superior position placed an unsustainable burden on their already faltering economy. Thus, military superiority, the master role, became economically impossible for them. This, plus the growing discontent of the masses within Russia and its satellite states, led to the downfall of the Soviet system and the end of the Cold War.

This is a story of good conflict with an unreasonable nation. The Cold War ended not because the U.S. was nice but because the U.S. was strong. It's not that the Soviets became reasonable, but that they became realistic. They changed because internal pressures made holding to their system no longer feasible. We didn't change their minds; we changed the conditions. And when the conditions changed, they changed their minds. Good conflict was achieved because the U.S. did two things: set relational boundaries and acknowledged relational realities.

Setting Relational Boundaries

With reasonable people we solve problems by working together to reach mutually satisfying solutions. Reasoning with reasonable people works, which makes for good conflict. But it doesn't work with unreasonable people because they don't have the necessary "reason muscles." And if we attempt it, the frustration we experience puts us right back into their drama.

Reasoning doesn't work, but a limited substitute does—setting boundaries. Boundaries accomplish what reasoning can't. He tried everything he could to convince the neighbor to leash the mutt but nothing worked. Finally he improved the situation by putting up a fence. In this case, the solution that couldn't be achieved through reasoning was achieved through boundaries. Yes, it cost him something, but it worked. With reasonable people, problems are solved when both sides participate in the reasoning process. With unreasonable people, problems are "restrained" when the reasonable person does a good job of setting boundaries.

A gentle reminder: All aspects of dealing with unreasonable people—assessing them, avoiding their dramas, accepting the limits—are challenging. So challenging, in fact, that we won't succeed without the support of others. Unreasonable people can be so confounding, so determined, and so frustrating that we'll fail if we try to go it alone. The understanding and reinforcement of other reasonable people is not a luxury but a necessity. Slaves in the pre-Civil War South understood this well. For all practical purposes, their masters operated under this unreasonable set of assumptions: "We're good, you're bad, you exist for us. If you submit to our control, we'll get along just fine." Lack of submission led to physical harm. Their sufferings under that system of chattel slavery were eased somewhat by singing songs that came to be known as "Negro Spirituals." Through the lyrics, they expressed thoughts and feelings to each other about their trials, their tribulations, and their hopes. The ability to endure was enhanced through mutual encouragement.

We may not be literally enslaved by unreasonable people, but the need for support is just as essential. Remember, the unreasonable person believes his survival depends upon getting us to believe "There's nothing wrong with him, but there's definitely something wrong with us." Without reference points for our sanity that others provide, it's very easy to get swept into that distortion and become discouraged. *Good conflict with unreasonable people is achievable only with the support of reasonable people relationships.*

Let's look now at principles involved in setting relational boundaries with each of the three levels of unreasonable people.

Setting Boundaries with Level 1 (Dormant) Unreasonable People

Left to himself, the Level 1 unreasonable person doesn't change. But when the person he needs to entice into the drama refuses to cooperate, it creates conflict pressure. And if the pressure is high enough, he displays a surprising capacity to grow, which is why the word *dormant* is used. Our goal with a Level 1 unreasonable person is to use boundaries that promote *growth*.

We can't make growth happen, but we can create conditions under which growth is more likely to occur. The experience of dealing with a Level 1 unreasonable person is very similar to that of being a toddler's parent, an elementary schoolteacher, or a coach. It takes a lot of work, but the outcome is worth the effort. We have to be frustrating, persistent, and patient.

Be Frustrating

By advising you to be frustrating, I don't mean that we are to be maliciously hurtful. I do mean that we should intentionally frustrate the drama process by refusing to play our designated roles so the resulting discomfort gives the unreasonable person an incentive to grow. That's what happened in the grocery store checkout line when Penny refused to participate in the verbal tug of war with our daughter. When it became clear to our little girl that she couldn't get Penny to play her part, she was forced to grow up a little. Refusing roles such as subservience, gratefulness, rescuing, or pretending discombobulates the unreasonable person, making him feel uncomfortable. But that's good because that feeling may cause him or her to seek out more mature ways of relating.

Chapter 6: Changing Your Environment

Prioritize Your Relationships

Have you ever noticed that the older we get, the busier we become? Each year that passes brings new opportunities, new challenges, and new relationships. It's not like hundreds of people suddenly come into our lives. But each new commitment or relationship adds to the ones we already have until we feel inundated:

Someone recommends a book that's exactly what we were looking for.

We hear about a "must visit" restaurant that's opened.

An old friend connects with us through social media.

New opportunities at church promise personal growth and outreach.

We begin a new relationship that we want to nurture.

A promotion at work provides a bump in pay but greater responsibility.

We're taking classes toward a degree and have to do extensive homework.

Growing kids means growing demands on our time, energy, and sanity.

Notice the common thread: these are all *good* things. It's not like we're subscribing to the vice-of-the-month club. These are all things we believe can make our life richer, so we want to add them all.

The problem is that we add new activities without getting rid of any old ones. We're not replacing good commitments with better ones; we're simply making a longer list. When we have trouble giving the proper level of attention to each one, we feel guilty.

Marco described his dilemma several weeks ago while attending one of my seminars. He's a seasoned musician, composer, and recording artist, having spent the past fifteen years on concert stages around the world. Now he wants to shift gears and invest in young musicians, using his own experience to mentor them on their career paths.

"I've made a lot of relationships around the world over those years," he said, "and I don't want to give them up. But if I move in this new direction, it's going to take a lot of time and energy. I'll be developing new relationships as this new focus takes off. So how do I build new quality relationships while still maintaining the old ones?"

That's a real dilemma. Most of us face some version of that every day. We add new but we don't want to subtract old. Soon our closets, garages, file cabinets, and even our minds become stuffed to the point that we feel out of control.

To find a good solution, we have to accept one absolute, irrefutable, undeniable fact:

Time is limited. We only have twenty-four hours in a day.

Opportunity Cost

As long as we believe we can do everything and have it all, we'll never solve the problem of being overcommitted. We'll take time management seminars and read self-help books to find ways to cram more into our lives. Those will actually help for a while, but it's like rearranging the deck chairs on the *Titanic*. It may look better, but it won't keep the ship from going down.

We might think of a person we know who gets more done than us. It's easy to think, "Well, they must have more time than I do." But they have twenty-four hours, just like we have twenty-four hours. Somehow, they're more productive than we are.

However, there's a greater problem. It doesn't matter if we're doing *more* things if we're not doing the *right* things.

In economics, the concept is called "opportunity cost." It means that whatever you say yes to, you're automatically saying no to everything else at that time. If you spend an hour in a meeting, you're not exercising, cleaning, or reading during that time. If you're talking to a friend on the phone, you're giving up the opportunity to wash your car. If you take the kids to Disneyland, you're not mowing the lawn.

Those are all good things, but we can only do one thing at a time. Since time is limited, we can't do everything. The only way to survive is to prioritize our choices, deciding which ones would be the best use of our time.

Suppose your house caught on fire and you knew it would be engulfed in flames within minutes. What would you take with you as you ran out the door? Almost everyone gives the same answer: the things that have the most value. The list usually consists of family members, pets, photo albums, and other irreplaceable items. No one rushes back into a burning house to get their favorite mug.

Relationship Cost

The more value something has to us, the more careful we are. That's why we try not to drop our laptop or balance a glass of lemonade on the keyboard.

That principle applies to our relationships as well. We might have a lot of relationships we enjoy, and we value the uniqueness of each connection. But we're limited in the amount of time and energy we have available. When we spend time with one person, we're giving up the opportunity to spend time with someone else. Though it might sound heartless, we need to prioritize our relationships, spending appropriate amounts of time with different people based on their value in our lives.

My wife Diane is more important to me than anyone on the planet. I have a lifelong commitment to her, which means I need to invest most heavily in that relationship. I also have a career and have discovered that certain people tend to think that I should show up. My job is a valuable part of my life and requires a solid chunk of time and commitment. But that takes time away from Diane.

Sometimes I travel, so I'm gone for several days at a time. When that happens, I don't get to spend time with my wife. When I return home, there are many people I could catch up with. But even though those are good relationships, I've learned the value of investing in Diane first. I might change jobs or locations or other situations, but I'm not planning on changing wives.

No Guarantees

Alison goes to the gym four times a week. She joined a spin class and a yoga class. She doesn't eat red meat, grows her own vegetables, and drinks purified water. She takes supplements and wears sunscreen.

Patrick eats bacon four times a week. He watches weight-loss reality shows on television while eating chips. His weight lifting program consists of standing up. He eats mayonnaise from the jar with his fingers. He has installed a soda tap in his garage.

So, who's going to live the longest?

Alison has taken every precaution to protect her health, but she could get hit by a texting driver while walking through a parking lot. Patrick could defy the odds and live to be a hundred.

Is it fair? No. There are no guarantees in life. We plan for the worst but hope for the best. Neither Alison nor Patrick can control every aspect of their lives. Normally, our choices determine our outcomes; but the outcomes are not guaranteed. The only things we have control over are the choices, not the results.

How Long Before My Crazy People Change?

We can only change ourselves. If we think that by hanging in there long enough they'll come around, we'll probably be disappointed. The only way we can avoid being a victim is to make the right choices because those choices are right, not because they might convince someone to change.

It's hard to stay motivated when our crazy person doesn't change. Our willpower runs out, our tank runs dry, and we think, "When will things get better?"

There are no guarantees. It might not get better. They might never change. The only way we can be drama-free in our relationships is to focus on us, not them. We're the ones who can change.

Making healthy choices in our relationships isn't a one-time decision that lasts forever. To stay motivated, we have to keep making those choices day by day, over and over.

Relationships Don't Come with Guarantees

A guarantee is a promise that something will perform as expected. We buy a new car or appliance and we expect it to do what the brochure promised. If that doesn't happen, the manufacturer will either fix it or replace it. Most people won't make a major purchase without that type of guarantee.

Wouldn't it be great if relationships came with guarantees? Any time someone in our lives got crazy, we could call up the store and trade them in for a better model. "I'm sorry," we would say, "this one isn't working. I think we have a lemon. When can I bring him back?"

Life doesn't work that way, however. Like a used car, our relationships come "as is." When something goes wrong, we can try to fix it or work around it. But no matter what we do, the other person might stay broken (which implies that we're *not* broken). In our society it's common for people to quickly discard relationships when they don't live up to expectations, as evidenced by the high divorce rate. But if we're committed for the long haul, we have to distinguish between the things we can change and the things we can't change.

What can we *not* change? Other people. What *can* we change? Ourselves. What do we do when the other person doesn't change? *Accept* (the reality of the situation) and *adapt* (change the way we think and respond).

The Bible is filled with passages that describe the need to take responsibility for ourselves rather than others.

"You, then, why do you judge your brother or sister? Or why do you treat them with contempt?" (verse 10)

"Each of us will give an account of ourselves to God." (verse 12)

"Let us stop passing judgment on one another." (verse 13)

The principle is simple: We are only responsible for our own choices and actions. We're not responsible for the choices of others.

So, What's My Job?

If you've had teenagers, you've probably experienced the dilemma. It's our responsibility to guide our kids as they grow into adulthood, and we provide boundaries to steer them in the right direction. The purpose is to help them become responsible adults, being able to function independently and make wise decisions. The older they get, the more the responsibility for those choices transfers from us to them.

Yesterday I went to a park near our house. As I sat by the lake, I watched a family of ducks swimming near the shoreline. The parents swam with one of their ducklings while the second duckling paddled off by itself in a different direction. Soon, several other ducks surrounded the duckling in what appeared to be a threatening way. The duckling began to panic.

The mother left her family and moved toward the group until the other ducks moved away. She then guided her duckling gently back to her family.

Once they were back together, she pecked the little duck so hard he completely submerged in the water. As soon as he came back up, she did it again. He barely broke the surface before it happened a third time.

When to Leave

At forty, Jim has spent his entire career in the banking industry. He knows his way around banking like the back of his hand and could talk about finances in his sleep (and probably does). He's competent in his skills and confident in his abilities.

Over the years, Jim has worked at several different banking institutions. Good situations, bad situations—he's seen it all. But his last job stretched him to the limit. In his position as director of operations, he had responsibility for a large part of the organization. The bank was struggling, and Jim knew his input could move it back onto solid ground.

The problem was his boss. Usually, bosses are supposed to remove barriers for their employees, freeing them up to use their unique strengths to excel in their work. But this manager *was* the barrier. He wouldn't listen to Jim's ideas and micromanaged every detail of his position. Jim began to feel devalued and became discouraged and depressed about his situation.

Jim knew he couldn't continue this way long-term. Sure, he could have stormed into his boss's office and yelled, "I can't take it anymore. You're crazy! I quit." But he knew that would be a reactive response and he would regret the consequences of that choice.

First, he tried to change the situation. He used logic, influence, and careful confrontation to change the dynamics of the relationship. He asked businesspeople he respected how they would handle things. He focused on supporting and affirming his superiors. But over time, nothing changed.

Second, he worked on his attitude. Convinced that the situation wouldn't change, Jim realized he could be a victim or a victor. It was easy to be a victim, letting his emotions be controlled by the environment he was in. That's where he began, feeling hopeless and mentally disengaging from his work. But input from caring friends was the catalyst for change. Instead of being a victim, he realized that for now, this was his job. He decided to focus on being dedicated, learning whatever he could from the bad situation while he was still there. He reengaged with his company, giving it his best effort in spite of the people around him. "The turning point," he said, "was when I remembered that I was really working for God, not for these people."

During that time, Jim took the third step: change his environment. He knew it wouldn't be healthy to stay in that situation long-term, so he started looking for a new opportunity. In a tight economy, it seemed like an uphill climb. But with consistent steps, he explored different opportunities while giving 100 percent in his current position. Several months later, he found a new position in a new industry.

The result was the same: he changed jobs. But it wasn't a knee-jerk reaction. He followed a three-step process to ensure the best outcome:

1. Change the situation
2. Change your attitude
3. Change your environment

Jim grew through the process and was able to have a healthy attitude when he left his previous employer.

Our situation may involve different people, but the scenario is the same. Whether it's an unreasonable boss, interfering parents, a demanding spouse, undisciplined kids, nosy neighbors, insensitive friends, or crazy siblings, someone else's choices are creating havoc in our lives.

Sometimes we feel hopeless. We're trapped in a job or a relationship and don't see any way out:

- "I'm a single parent, and I can't quit my job."
- "My spouse is abusive, but I don't have anywhere to go."
- "My sister is driving me crazy, but you can't divorce your sister."
- "My parents stick their nose into everything I do, but I can't disrespect them."
- "If I confront them or end the relationship, they'll explode—and I don't think I'm ready for that."

These situations all involve people we care about. In fact, that's why they're driving us crazy. Someone we work with could show the same behaviors and we would think it was entertaining. But when it's someone we care about and we feel stuck with them, the situation seems hopeless.

When the tension builds, we wonder how much longer we can put up with it. Everything inside us wants to run away and escape the situation.

So, is leaving a bad thing?

In most cases, it's bad if it's a reactive response. But if it's the last resort of a carefully thought-out process, it could be the healthiest solution.

Should I Leave or Stay?

Since every situation is different, we can't have a one-size-fits-all checklist. That would be handy, but there are as many solutions as there are situations. Generally, all of the solutions fit into one of three actions:

1. Stay in a bad situation
2. Leave a bad situation
3. Stay in a bad situation with a strategy for working on it

Stay in a Bad Situation

Staying in a bad situation *with no plan for changing the situation or our response* is almost always a bad idea. Ignoring the problems we face won't make them go away. We hope things will get better and that our crazy person will change.

Yes, it's possible—but so is winning the lottery. We know the chances of winning big are almost nonexistent, but we keep buying tickets "just in case."

Why do people stay in bad situations? There could be a number of reasons:

- They're afraid of what the crazy person will do if they quit the job or end the relationship.
- They're afraid of what will happen to them if they pull out.
- They're afraid of what other people will say.

- They're afraid of the unknown.
- They've always been a victim, so they don't know any other way of living.
- They listen to advice from well-meaning friends who are trying to fix them.
- They're afraid of conflict.
- They're trying to protect the crazy person.

Most of those reasons have to do with *fear*. That might seem unreasonable, but people have an emotional set point within any situation where the pain is more comfortable than the prospect of the unknown. That's why people often stay in jobs with an abusive boss: it's all they know, whereas taking positive steps is risky.

One of the most dangerous reasons to stay in a bad situation is trying to protect the crazy person. We make excuses for their behavior because we don't want people to think badly of them or because they embarrass us. The problem is that when we protect them, we shield them from the negative consequences of their behavior. If they don't have consequences, they never have an incentive to change. They might apologize and promise things will be different, but promises have to be backed up with performance. Blind loyalty on our part can actually keep healing from happening.

Staying in a bad situation without any plan for change is like constantly putting air in a leaky tire without patching the hole.

Leave a Bad Situation

Leaving should be a calculated choice, making it the last resort after all other options have been exhausted. It might involve quitting a job, changing churches, or moving from a toxic friendship. Leaving too quickly and impulsively rids us of the uncomfortable situation but doesn't resolve the issues that led to the problem in the first place.

Every relationship problem involves interaction between two or more people. The crazy person may be primarily at fault, but we need to consider our contribution as well—how we respond, what we say, the choices we make. If we aren't being realistic by recognizing the reality of our part in the problem, we'll carry those same responses and attitudes into the next situation.

"OK," you say, "I've tried everything possible to change the situation, and it won't budge. They're still crazy. I've worked on my attitude and response, but I'm running out of ammunition. At what point should I consider a change?"

Again, there are no absolutes. But here are the questions to ask yourself:

- Am I unable to keep from being a victim?

- Do I see myself as less of a person because of the other person's choices?
- Am I (or the people I'm responsible for) in danger?
- What, exactly, will I be giving up if I leave?
- What, exactly, will it cost me to stay?
- If I leave, what steps can I take to genuinely resolve these questions?

If you answered yes to any of the first three questions, that doesn't necessarily mean you should make a change. But when added to your answers to the last three questions, it provides the foundation for making a careful decision.

Stay in the Situation, but with a Plan

There's a big difference between staying in a bad situation with no plan and staying with a carefully crafted blueprint. The first is wishful thinking; the second provides genuine hope.

If we make the choice to stay, it shouldn't be because we feel obligated to "hang in there." It should be because we've determined that there is (a) sufficient value in the relationship to make it worth the effort, and (b) sufficient evidence that the other person is willing to participate in the change. If they're not willing to work on it, they won't see any consequences, which means there will be no change. We don't want to impulsively quit a dysfunctional job without something else lined up, but we become victims if we stay without a course of action for improving the situation.

It takes effort to make a blueprint for relationships. It's not quite as hard with casual, irritating relationships. With a spouse or family member, getting help from a professional counselor could be a valuable resource for charting a new course. In any case, the plan needs to design ways of coping with our anger and hurt when it happens, as well as strategies for dealing with painful issues as they arise. We also need a clear delineation of physical and emotional boundaries for the other person. "Good fences make good neighbors," as Robert Frost said. If we're going to stay, we need a plan.

Staying Power

If we decide to stay in a situation, committing energy to make it work, here are suggestions to survive and thrive:

- Think through your options. Be sure that the plan is in place before making the decision.
- Decide what your nonnegotiables are if you stay—the boundaries that will keep the plan on task.
- Find a way to be yourself in the relationship. Pretending that you're OK can drain your energy over time and keep the relationship from growing.

- Base everything on truth. Be willing to set aside your fears, prejudices, and inaccurate lenses to see things the way they really are. Look at the facts behind the feelings.
- Look at the time you remain in the relationship as a test period where you both work on how you relate to each other. That provides a chance to evaluate evidence of growth or decay. If things fail to progress, go back to the decision-making process about staying or leaving.
- It's never healthy to be a martyr. Don't base your identity on the fact that you're hanging in there in a debilitating relationship.
- Take ownership of your decision. Recognize that there will be no perfect choice, because every decision has good and bad outcomes. Instead of trying to make exactly the right choice, make a healthy choice and then make it right.
- Let the other person take ownership of their side of the relationship. We need to take care of ourselves and let them take care of themselves. Instead of rescuing them, we need to let them make their choices and reap the consequences of those choices.

Committing to a Decision

Write down the names of three people you have the most challenging relationship with and why. Rank them based on their level of challenge. Take the top one and ask: What would be the worst thing that would happen if I *left* this relationship? What would be the best thing? What would be the worst thing that would happen if I *stayed* in this relationship? What would be the best thing?

Then show the list to a trusted, objective friend to evaluate if you're seeing clearly or if your own lens is distorted.

There are no easy answers, but looking at our relationships with eyes wide open, we can evaluate and make decisions with wisdom.

Staying in a toxic relationship without a plan is a dangerous choice. Wavering in our decision making isn't healthy either. We might choose to leave, or we might choose to stay. Staying in the middle is a recipe for disaster.

Chapter 7: The "Anti-Difficult People" Toolkit and How To Learn from It

The "Anti-Difficult People" Toolkit

As you go through life, you will, time and again, be faced with one or several difficult people -- at work, at school or sometimes, at home. What do you do?

Listen Carefully. Instinct will tell you to shut your ears and not let these people get to you. This can sometimes be good, but if you're shooting for a long-term defense, you'll want to be aware of who or what you're dealing with.

The thing with difficult people is that more often than not, they simply need to be understood. Difficult people succeed or become worse when people react negatively to them. When you turn to give them your fullest attention - even for just a moment - you end up giving them what they want, making them less hostile, even if it's just for a day.

Besides, everybody likes a good listener. When you make these people your friends, it becomes easier for you to reach out to them.

Don't Be Hasty. Remember how difficult people thrive in the way people react? When you encounter these people, try not to give in to your instincts. Stop first, and think about how you will react. By doing so, you are able to take control of the situation because you get to decide what course of action to take. It only takes a few seconds of your time to think about what you should do in order to save your entire day.

Remember to Put Yourself First. Taking the time to do something to help difficult people can be a noble act, but don't ever do it at the cost of your own well being. Sometimes we get so caught up in the "selfless act" of pleasing these people to appease them, but you end up losing more respect, not only from yourself, but also from the other people around you. Sometimes you have to put your foot down and disagree with these difficult people, not because it's the best way to go, but because the damage they can do to your self-esteem would be a bigger blow.

Remember, you can't help others if you don't help yourself first.

Laugh. There are experiences in life that you would one day look back to and laugh. Why not make this one the kind you would just laugh at today? Encountering difficult people can be seen as a bad experience, and they can be the kind you can just laugh about.

Of course, this is not to say that you should laugh at these people. That's just mean. But what you should do is to laugh at the reality that some people are just the way they are. In these instances, the right perspective is your best defense.

As the old saying goes, "don't take life too seriously, because nobody ever gets out of it alive."

Don't Blame Yourself. Nothing in this world is ever within your complete control. Corollary to #4, keep in mind that sometimes, bad things just happen. And when things go bad, and everybody gets mad, you need to secure yourself the truth that will keep you sane: that it's not your fault (assuming, of course, that it is not your fault), and that someone was just being difficult.

This mindset is particularly important for those difficult people that you just can't live with anymore. It will be your key to moving on from a toxic relationship or quitting the employment of a control freak boss.

These five tips are pretty basic. If you master them, you're already halfway there.

Avoiding the Pitfalls During Interaction

You've learned the do's. Now here are the don'ts:

Do Not Generalize Difficult People. The worst thing that you could do to a difficult person is to always assume he or she is up to no good. When you look at a difficult person and say "oh, it's him/her again," you're not different from someone who just ignores that person.

Sometimes we forget that these people are good for something too. If he or she is a co-worker, there has to be a reason why he or she is there, right?

For example, what if the control freak actually is an expert at a specific task that he or she is taking command? Should you deny control just because the person is a control freak?

Or what if the toxic person really does have a good reason to be angry for once? Are you going to just ignore the rants because Mr. Toxic is just being Mr. Toxic again?

Do Not Be Mean. They are the difficult ones, not you. Sure they have issues, but they are otherwise normal, imperfect people, just like you. Every now and then their bad side will rear its ugly head, but you should be nice to them on any other day. These people are still family or friend too, and developing some kind of festering dislike towards them is just going to make YOU as bad as them.

They are difficult people, not impossible. So what? That doesn't mean you have to be too. Don't be a baby about it and be mature when you relate with these people.

Do Not Underestimate Their Potential. Studies have shown that people with personality disorders can be really smart or very competitive people. This could be the case with most difficult people.

For instance, the narcissists can be very competitive and ambitious, which means that they are likely to do their best when entrusted with work. If you look beyond the ugly parts, the pessimists or even the toxic people can be good sources of criticism (assuming you learn to sift through the negative comments).

Since you can't get rid of these people, you might as well find ways to be able to benefit from them, right? Plus, by tapping their positive side, you can help them feel more secure about themselves, which can do wonders even for the most difficult people.

Learning from Difficult People

There's always something you can learn from others, and that includes the difficult people too. Sometimes it's so tough to look beyond the facade of being difficult that we forget that we can get something good out of them as well. Here are some of the values we can get from someone who is being difficult:

Self-awareness. Remember how you always have to be in tune with your emotions so you can prepare yourself for difficult people? That requires a lot of self-awareness, which is a very useful life skill.

Self-control. Yes, this is a very obvious value that you can learn from this type of folks. In fact, it goes hand-in-hand with self-awareness. And the best part about learning self-control is that it branches out to other life skills, such as tolerance and patience.

Forgiveness. You are definitely going to learn to create and give out a lot of this when you know how to cope with difficult people. Seeing as how aggression should never be a resort in most cases, you're going to need to let go of a lot of damage that difficult people could potentially do. Of course, this does not mean that you should go to the extent of saying that it's okay for people to bully or exploit your kindness. But, more often than not, you're going to want to just let go and learn from each experience, since there's no point in crying over spilled milk.

Compassion. The thing about understanding a person is that it requires you to genuinely be concerned with another person's welfare. When you take time to understand a person better, you get to see how much help that person needs. As you step into another's shoes, you will be more aware that these people just need a bit of care and understanding.

These are just some of the things you can pick up from even the most difficult of people. But the more important part is that all these values you develop from coping with difficult people are actually essential to most of your daily living. Whether you're looking to get better at your job or want to make more friends, these qualities can only help you become better at facing other challenges in day to day living.

Learning to Avoid Becoming a Difficult Person

Perhaps the most unique lesson you can learn from difficult people is how not to become difficult yourself. When you see how other people behave negatively, you get a really good example of how not to relate with other people.

These encounters can give you an opportunity to reflect upon yourself: are you prone to doing the same things you've disliked someone else for?

Chapter 8: Expert Techniques to Deal with Difficult People

Practice reflective listening

Have you ever been upset, and then someone comes in and tells you, "I understand," Did that ever make you feel better?

I didn't think so!

Well, one thing that is important to note is that using such kind of statements will not help you accomplish anything. Let us consider an instance where you have a client in your company. They tell you that they are frustrated because of the budget cuts and the fact that you are not willing to offer them discounts even though they have been your loyal clients for several years. How do you respond to that? Do you just tell them that you understand what they are going through?

The truth is that if you did tell them you understand, that conversation is probably never going to have a good ending.

If you are in such a tight spot with a difficult client, the first thing you should tell yourself is to practice reflective listening. In other words, try to put yourself in the other person's shoes. Understand what it is that they are saying by simply interpreting their body language and words. This will help you to respond by reflecting their thoughts and emotional feelings back to them.

Instead of telling them plainly that you understand, try something like - "So, if I get you correctly, you are saying that our pricing is too high that is becoming a barrier to your business, right? – and because of the tight budget you are working with and the fact that we are not offering discounts. Is that right?"

If you have understood what they are telling you, simply move on with your conversation. However, if you have not yet understood what they are going through, ask them to give you more information so that you can understand their situation better. The trick here is for you to make them feel that you get where they are coming from and that you are concerned. They want to feel your empathy.

Try as much as you can to avoid making promises you know you might not be able to meet. The goal is to make the difficult person feel that they have been heard and that they are greatly valued.

Consider their affect heuristic

This simply refers to a mental shortcut. This plays a significant role in helping you make a quick and efficient decision based on your emotional feelings towards the other person, situation, and the place you are at. In simple terms, our choices are greatly influenced by our experiences and general outlook of the world around us. It is merely because of our bias.

The leading cause of the problem is that we are not objective in such situations, and facts do not matter that much. We choose to run every decision we make based on our mental software and then develop strong opinions based on that.

If the difficult person keeps having a different opinion and keeps asking you what you think is the catch, try not to respond rubbish them off by saying that we have to move on because of ABCD's. There is a chance that this person may be trapped in another information source, contract, or agreement with the previous vendor who failed to deliver what they had promised they would. Based on that very experience, they may be looking at you through the same lenses.

What you need to do is ask questions so that you fully understand what the root cause of the problem is. Some of the questions you can ask them so that they can relax and offer you insight as to why they are resistant include;

- I really would like to understand why you are a little skeptical about this. Would you tell me more?

- Is there anything we can do to relieve your fears?

- What can we do to help you feel comfortable enough so that we can all move forward?

When you ask such questions, you are allowing them to simply redirect their thoughts from thinking that you are not trustworthy in considering what is needed for the team to move forward and make progress.

Tap into the beginner's mind

The beginner's mind is often referred to like the Zen mind, and it serves as a strategy of approaching each situation as though you have no prior experience in it. Whenever you adopt this kind of thinking when dealing with a difficult person, every conversation you engage in is made with the "I don't know" mindset. This allows you to try as much as you cannot judge the other person or the situation.

This also goes a long way in helping you not to live with the 'should' kind of thinking. "You should have thought of the budget before the year started. You should have read my email concerning the discount expirations. You should have known that I am a busy person and available only once in a week for consultations."

When you are addressing a difficult person, try not to use 'should' statements. They only set your mind on the defensive and get in the way of your productivity and conversation before it can even start.

The good thing with adopting the Zen mindset is that it allows you to let go of an expert mindset. While you may be an expert in your field or in what you do, you have to realize that you are not an expert when it comes to a difficult person or situation.

For instance, instead of saying things like "You said that you wanted to increase your sales by 30% by the end of the month and the kind of delays am seeing will not make this possible," choose to approach the conversation in a beginner's mindset. Try not to prejudge the other person. Forget what it is that they should have done and perceive the conversation you are both having as a puzzle that needs to be solved.

You can choose to say something like this instead "It seems to me like with these delays, we will not be able to reach our sales goals. But, let's explore strategies that will help us achieve the results that we are aiming for." If you keenly study this statement, you will realize that you are acknowledging the fact that there is a problem, but immediately starts moving in the direction of a possible solution.

Let go of fear

Again, you cannot be afraid of negative results to the point that you allow that to drive your reactions. It is because of doubt that we tend to feel the need to control things and the people around us. If a colleague is difficult, you may feel afraid of challenging them because that might just put your relationship at risk. If a client expresses displeasure in your services, timelines, or pricing structure, you may be afraid because you think that you might not be able to fix the whole situation.

The first thing is to let go of the idea that there is something that needs fixing. When you are having a conversation with a difficult person – whether a friend, child, client, or coworker – remember that your role is to listen, understand what they are saying and then discern what the next steps forward should be. I don't mean that you start dishing out solutions immediately. Take time to go over what they have told you and then think through the possible solutions to find the best way forward.

For instance, rather than trying to validate emotional feelings, slap together common fixes, or apologizing, what you can do is express how unfortunate it is that the situation happened once again. Assure the other person that you get how the whole situation is affecting the business or your relationship and then appreciate them for being patient enough to allow you to work towards resolving the issue.

"Chunk" the problem

You may be wondering what 'chunking' is all about. Well, this simply refers to the process of taking a huge problem and then breaking it down into smaller manageable portions that you can address one at a time. When you break problems into smaller portions, this allows you to handle them. They also make people more willing to start dealing with all the issues at hand.

What I have learned from my mentor over the years is the importance of chunking things and then organizing them into tasks that you can handle every other day. This is the same way you can choose to deal with a tough situation with a difficult person.

Does your employee always find a reason not to turn in their work on time because they cannot get started using the new software?

What you can do is to ask them to help you break down each of the steps into smaller bite-size pieces that you can work on to come up with an easy to follow protocol. The point is for you not to apportion blame or say that they are lazy, but to find the best way forward. When each task is chunked, it becomes easier for the other person to digest what is left to be done.

Remember, anger is natural

We have all encountered difficult people – clients, friends, and colleagues alike – that we get so furious. It could also be that you have been on the other side of things. For instance, if you are a customer at a store and you pay for a new product upgrade, and then you realize that it is shallow that it makes you angry.

The recalibration theory of anger states that anger is a natural emotion that is wired into human beings. In other words, you have to realize that anger is the best way we have been made to get into the bargain. We press our lips together, bite our tongue, furrow our brows, or flare our nostrils just so that we can drive the other person to a place of higher value based on what we have to give.

If you are dealing with a difficult person, the point is for you to try and avoid justifying your actions or position. Realize that the reason why they could be feeling that way is that they think that their opinion is being undervalued or that they want to control the situation. It is advisable that you take the other person's frustrations seriously and not personally. Once you have understood the frustrations and arguments of the other person, thank them for bringing that to your attention. Also, let them know that you will think through everything and get back to them with a solution or a way forward.

When the other person is already furious, the chances are that they will not take any solution you offer at that time. However right the answer might be, they will not feel like it is the best way to go about the whole situation. Therefore, you must allow them some time to calm down before you can pick up the discussions where you left them – this time, with practicality and reason.

But what if the difficult person is already raging with anger, how can you deal with the situation?

Well, there are so many ways you can try to calm the whole situation down;

Keep your calm

This is probably a point you will see everywhere in this book – because it is essential and easy to get wrong. If someone sends you an angry text or email or starts shouting at you on the phone, the truth is that it is hard not to get personal. There is a chance that you will get a bristle of anger, and defensive thoughts will begin to pop into your mind of how wrong you think the other person is. You will start to think about how ungrateful they are for all the hard work you give the company, and before you know it, you are exploding with fury.

The best thing to do is to take in a deep breath. Try to take in what it is that the other person is trying to say. In between those lines, you might note that the other person is in a struggle or is frustrated with the whole process, product or service to the point that they took it out on you or the team. We are all human, and there are times when we are caught in our moments of weakness. If you try to understand this fact, you will not see the reason why you should take their difficulty, comments, or arguments personally or hold it against them.

If the other person is being abusive, rude, or aggressive in their language or intonation, don't tolerate their behavior. If, at some point during the conversation, you feel like they are belittling you, simply feel free to escalate the situation to a third-party that can help you resolve without killing the other.

Let us consider an instance where a client calls the support team in your company expressing how upset they are about the delay in the delivery of their products. They may be agitated and are shouting at the top of their lungs on the phone call. This is where your support team or you should remain calm and try to ask the three what's; what is the problem, what are their goals, needs or desires, and what are the available options. If you are the one on the other side of the phone, keep your cool and find out more details about their issue. That alone will work to de-escalate an angry person.

Practice active listening

Try as much as you can to focus on what they are saying - rather than the anger behind their words and voice. When your attention is on what they are really saying, you will be better placed to determine what it is that is agitating them. This will also help you resolve the issue rather than trying only to de-escalate it to comfort them. When you know what the problem is, you can find a solution, and you will have a satisfied colleague, friend, or client at the end of the day.

Let us consider an instance where a client walks into your store and tells you that the product you sold them stopped working for them a few days after they bought it. They continue to tell you how surprised and disappointed that you could offer such a poorly designed product.

What will you do? What will your response be like?

Well, the simplest way to go is to pay attention to the words they use – surprised, disappointed. Those are the words they used to express their emotional feelings. The point is that they are not angry but surprised by how your product behaved.

In such an instance, you may be tempted to respond with the words "I understand that you are frustrated..." while that is a response, it is not only going to escalate the other person's feelings but will now make them angry. By saying that, you are only giving them a reason to go from disappointment and surprise to anger.

However, if you demonstrate that you are actively listening to what they have to say, you will calm the situation down. You can say things like "that is certainly surprising and disappointing. Let me take a look to know why the product stopped working unexpectedly." With this response, you are acknowledging the client's feelings without necessarily escalating them.

Repeat back what your customers say

One of the key components of active listening is ensuring that your client and you are on the same page. Once you know the root cause of their anger, you can simply repeat what you heard from them so that you are sure you understand what is making them angry. In so doing, you are also letting the other person know that you get hat their concerns are and are working on a resolution or response.

Let us consider an instance where someone badges into your office ranting about the product you sold them not working. You can simply start your response with such words as "What am hearing you say is…" this will simply get the ball rolling. Try to highlight how the issue is standing in the way of them achieving their goals. This will show them that you did not just listen but understood their needs and are going to help them.

Conclusion

Indeed, dealing with difficult people is one of the toughest tasks in life. They are the kind of people who will ruin your perfect day before it can even begin. It could be a colleague, family member, partner, or friend. It could also be anyone random you run into at the street. Whoever that may be, the trick is to ensure that you have armed yourself with the above methods, steps, and approaches to deal with them appropriately.

Realize that difficult people exist all around us, and if you don't do something about them, then you risk letting them hurt others.

The truth is that there is no easy way to deal with these people – after all, they are different combinations of personality traits. They all have different ways to make others' life difficult.

As the saying goes, "It takes two to tango." Realize that these difficult people may not even notice that they are difficult. To most of them, this is their usual way of life. In fact, to a difficult person, everyone else around them is difficult. They don't have your perspective of things.

So, have you been continually dealing with difficult people yourself? If so, it might be time for you to take a look at your behavior. Ask yourself whether you are the one being difficult. Look for such indicators as;

- Lack of close connections at home, school or the workplace

- You lack a sense of self-worth in what you do

- You find yourself being misunderstood too often or complaining about this or that

- You always think that people are talking ill of you

- You still are an emotional person

- You feel like people don't even care or remember you

You might just be the difficult person we have been discussing here. If that is the case, then it is high time you use the strategies above to deal with your behavior. If these traits are what you see in someone around you, then you can also use the techniques we have discussed to help them become a better person.

Remember, a little self-reflection goes a long way in helping us be a better person to the people working and interacting with us daily.

You can help yourself and the difficult person around you to see what they are doing so that they can change for the long-term.

It is a win for all of us!

So, what are you waiting for? Start identifying them around you and help them BECOME!

www.ingramcontent.com/pod-product-compliance
Lightning Source LLC
Chambersburg PA
CBHW071415210526
45465CB00001B/392